HOW TO SURVIVE
THE NEW
MILLENNIUM

HOW TO SURVIVE THE NEW MILLENNIUM

Recycled Wisdom
For an Age of Diminished Expectations

Compiled by

HY BRETT
ILLUSTRATED BY RAY ALMA

ℬ

BRETT BOOKS
BROOKLYN, NEW YORK

Copyright © 1995 by Hy Brett.

Published in the United States of America by Brett Books, Inc., Box 290-637, Brooklyn, New York 11229-0011.

Library of Congress Cataloging-in-Publication Data

How to survive the new millennium : recycled wisdom for an age of diminished
    expectations / compiled by Hy Brett ; illustrated by Ray Alma.
        p.   cm
    ISBN 0-9636620-3-1 (alk. paper)
        1. Quotations, English.   2. Quotations.   I. Brett, Hy.
PN6081.H687   1995
082—dc20   95-5856

First Edition
Manufactured in the United States of America
Printed on acid-free paper

95 96 97 98 99 00   10 9 8 7 6 5 4 3 2 1

Book design by C. Linda Dingler

DEDICATED TO

PRESIDENT JIMMY CARTER
PRESIDENT RONALD REAGAN
PRESIDENT GEORGE BUSH
PRESIDENT BILL CLINTON
THE U.S. CONGRESS
THE FEDERAL RESERVE BANK
THE DEMOCRATIC PARTY
THE REPUBLICAN PARTY

WHO BROUGHT US DOUBLE-DIGIT INFLATION
VOODOO ECONOMICS
SUPPLY-SIDE ECONOMICS
TRICKLE -DOWN ECONOMICS
THE TAX REFORM ACT OF 1984
THE TAX REFORM ACT OF 1986
DEREGULATION OF THE SAVINGS AND LOAN INDUSTRY
THE NORTH AMERICAN FREE TRADE AGREEMENT
THE GENERAL AGREEMENT ON TARIFFS AND TRADE

THE NOBLEST MOTIVE IS THE PUBLIC GOOD.
VIRGIL

A CREED FOR THE NEW MILLENNIUM

Be honest poverty thy boasted wealth;
So shall thy friendships be sincere tho' few,
So shall thy sleep be sound, thy waking cheerful.

William Havard

PREFACE

"To have nothing at all is not poverty," said Martial, the Roman author, in about the year 100, when bread and circuses were still free in Rome, and men and women were even entitled to a free workout with a lion if they were of the wrong religion or had offended the emperor or a senator. Though Rome lacked the blessings of democracy, its leaders were just as clever as any of our modern-day Democrats and Republicans, and their business enterprises in Gaul or Dacia were probably the inspiration for the savings and loan deals that, under the Reagan and Bush administrations, profited political insiders but will cost the rest of the us and our children and grandchildren almost a trillion dollars. "*Mutatis publicus screwandis*," as a Roman might say. Things change, but the public continues to get screwed.

But Rome's golden age of contentment lasted only another century, until the barbarians arrived and wouldn't leave, and ever since then, poverty has been getting an increasingly bad rap all over the world. I wish we had the time to proceed chronologically, beginning with St. Cyprian, bishop of Carthage, who said in *The World and Its Vanities* in about the year 250, "Man is bound fast by his gold, because his gold owns him rather than he owns it." Unfortunately, the subject is so urgent, and our economy so shaky, that we must leap the centuries and deal at once with America in the late nineties and then the new millennium.

This guide to surviving personal economic crisis was conceived on the day I lost my job as a freelance editor of western novels, including such classics as *Revenge at Rawhide* and *Guns on Fossil Ridge*. After the initial shock of being without income or a lead to another job, I did what any other sensible person in my situation would do, and I set out in search of a handy little book of quotations that would guide me through the uncertainties ahead.

Inside my local bookstore, famed throughout Brooklyn for its service and variety, I was unable to find a single work devoted to surviving without a job or income, which had become the fate of all too many Americans in the mid-nineties, and would, according to U.S. Secretary of Labor Robert B. Reich, engulf even more of us during the next millennium.

When I explained my problem to the proprietor, she said with a sad smile,

"I guess that just plain old survival is the one subject that has no positive aspects and therefore is not worthy of a book of quotations. What can you tell someone who has worked long and hard for an employer and then is dumped with an hour's notice?"

As a lifelong bibliophile and member in good standing of both the Brooklyn and New York public libraries, I could not and would not accept such a bleak assessment of the power of the printed word. I had found my mission.

Instead of knowing and reminding themselves daily of the joys and benefits of a lack of funds, all too many of the unemployed are starting to believe that to be poor is the end of the world. Let me assure these pessimists that my extensive research indicates that for most of us, at a certain time in our lives, being poor can be even *more satisfying than being rich*! (Italics and exclamation point suggested by Blair J. Sterling of the National Heritage Foundation for Macroeconomics and Human Values.) Or, at least, it can be a good place for us to reconsider our priorities, and to ponder whether the ladder of success is indeed worth the climb.

Therefore, as a guide to survival in our current economy, I have recycled the wisdom of the ages. Though said in other times and places, the observations are as relevant in these days of computers and cyberspace as in the days of quills and quadrilles.

Careful and frequent reading of this small book will surely bring you riches more desirable than mere money, because, as we learn from billionaire banker John D. Rockefeller, Jr., "Giving, and not having, is the secret of a healthy life."

When it comes to specifics, the opinions of the men and women quoted in this book are not necessarily the author's. For example, the lifestyle of St. Francis of Assisi makes poverty so attractive that readers may want to donate their savings to a foundation that will supply birdseed to deserving larks and sparrows. Before readers cash in their CDs or mutual funds, I urge them to consult with their spouse, parents, significant other, clergyman, guru, or shrink. Or at least their creditors and the IRS.

H.B.
Brooklyn, New York

ACKNOWLEDGMENTS

Some of the most memorable of these quotations were recycled from *Forty Thousand Quotations*, a noble work compiled by Charles Noel Douglas and published by the London firm of George G. Harrap & Company in 1916. Years ago, I bought the book for a dollar at a second-hand bookstore across the street from Van Cortlandt Park in the Bronx. I had gone to the bookstore in search of books by two of my wife, Barbara's, favorite authors, Will Cuppy and Thomas Hood.

The book of quotations was already old and fragile when I bought it, and while I was producing my own book in 1994, it often fell apart into many pieces. Barbara was always there in Brooklyn to help me repair it with tape, scissors, and either Elmer's or LePage's glue, whichever we were able to open first. Lacking eloquence, I will have to express my gratitude with a quote from William Cowper:

> What is there in the vale of life
> Half so delightful as a wife;
> When friendship, love and peace combine
> To stamp the marriage-bond divine?

HOW TO SURVIVE
THE NEW
MILLENNIUM

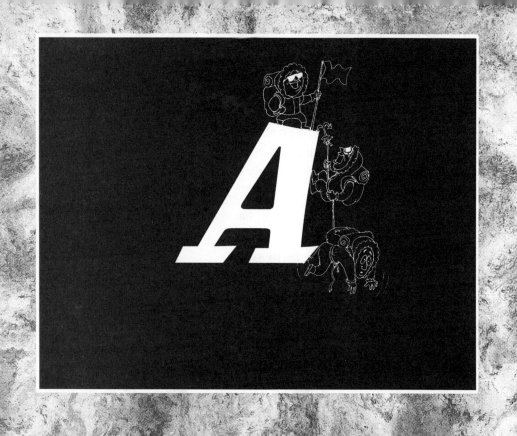

AARDVARK *See also*: OPPORTUNITY and SECOND CAREERS

There is so much activity in the world that everyone has a chance to be first at something, even if, like an aardvark, it's only on the page of a dictionary. ▶JESSICA WELLES

ABSTINENCE *See also*: LEAN AND MEAN

The more a man denies himself, the more he shall receive from God. ▶HORACE

ACTION *See also*: CORPORATE TAKEOVERS

Act well at the moment, and you have performed a good action for all eternity. ▶PEDRO CALDERON

ADAPTATION *See also*: PSYCHOTHERAPY

It is just as well to be a little giddy-pated if you are to feel at home on this turning earth. ▶LOGAN P. SMITH

ADMIRATION *See also*: PHOTO OPPORTUNITIES

The beauty that addresses itself to the eye is only a spell of the moment, because the eye of the body is not always that of the soul. ▶GEORGE SAND

ADOLESCENCE

Time cancels young pain. ▶EURIPIDES

ADVERSITY *See also:* GOLF and YACHTS

Adversity is the wholesome soil of virtue, where patience, honor, sweet humility and calm fortitude take root and strongly flourish.

▶DAVID MALLET

ADVICE *See also:* FINANCIAL ADVISERS, THERAPISTS and FIRST LADIES

Let no man value at a little price a virtuous woman's counsel; her winged spirit is feathered oftentimes with heavenly words.

▶GEORGE CHAPMAN

ALLERGIES *See also:* EARLY RETIREMENT and REJECTION

That which is painful to the body may be profitable to the soul. Sickness puts us in mind of our mortality, and while we drive on heedlessly in the full career of worldly pomp and jollity, it kindly pulls us by the ear and brings us to a proper sense of our duty.

▶RICHARD E. BURTON

AMBITION *See also*: FAST TRACK, THE

Most people would succeed in small things if they were not troubled by great ambitions. ▶LONGFELLOW

ANCESTORS *See also*: NEPOTISM and OLD BOY NETWORKS

I am no herald to inquire after men's pedigrees: it sufficeth me if I know of their virtues. ▶SIR PHILIP SIDNEY

ANGELS, GUARDIAN *See also*: GOLDEN PARACHUTES

The guardian angel of life sometimes flies so high that man cannot see it; but he always is looking down upon us, and will soon hover nearer to us. ▶JEAN PAUL RICHTER

ANTS *See also*: NETWORKING and SYNERGY

Forever toils the valiant ant,

Who never complains of wages scant.

When a worm crawls over for a little chat,

An ant won't pause to tip his hat.

▶BELINDA FORTESCUE

APPEARANCE AND REALITY *See also:* PUBLIC RELATIONS and SPIN DOCTORS

The bosom can ache beneath diamond brooches, and many a blithe heart dances under coarse wool. ▶EDWIN HUBBELL CHAPIN

The world is still deceived by ornament. ▶SHAKESPEARE

Deeds of lowly virtue fade before the glare of lofty ostentation. ▶F. G. KLOPSTOCK

APPENDICITIS *See also:* HEALTH PLAN, NATIONAL

Disease is the retribution of outraged Nature. ▶HOSEA BALLOU

APPLES *See also:* PARADISE, DEPRESSION, and BUSINESS CYCLES

The more we accommodate ourselves to plain things, and the less we indulge in those artificial delights which gratify pride and luxury, the nearer we approach to a state of innocency. ▶MATTHEW HENRY

APPOINTMENTS *See also:* JOB INTERVIEWS

Every man has his appointed day. ▶VIRGIL

APPRECIATION *See also*: COMPENSATION

It is a matter of the simplest demonstration that no man can be really appreciated but by his equal or superior. ▶JOHN RUSKIN

The applause of a single human being is of great consequence.
▶SAMUEL JOHNSON

ASPIRATION *See also*: FRUSTRATION

It seems to me that we can never give up longing and wishing while we are thoroughly alive. There are certainly things we feel to be beautiful and good, and we must hunger after them. ▶GEORGE SAND

No bird soars too high if he soars with his own wings. ▶WILLIAM BLAKE

ASSASSINATION *See also*: OP-ED PAGES

Assassination is not argument. ▶CASTELAR

ASTRONOMY *See also*: SUPERSTARS and FORTUNE COOKIES

If thou follow thy star, thou canst not fail of a glorious heaven.
▶DANTE

ATHEISM *See also:* SOCIAL SECURITY and RELIGION

An atheist is a man who has no invisible means of support.
▶ARCHBISHOP J. FULTON SHEEN

ATTIRE *See also:* JOB INTERVIEWS

Self-respect is the noblest garment with which a man may clothe himself.   ▶SAMUEL SMILES

An emperor in his nightcap will not meet with half the respect of an emperor in his crown.   ▶OLIVER GOLDSMITH

Beauty, like truth, never is so glorious as when it goes plainest.
▶LAURENCE STERNE

AUDITS, TAX

Poverty treads close upon the heels of great and unexpected wealth.

▶ANTOINE RIVAROL

AUTOMOBILES *See also:* REPOSSESSION

He travels safe, and not unpleasantly, who is guarded by poverty and guided by love.   ▶SIR PHILIP SIDNEY

AUTUMN *See also:* HOMELESSNESS and SHELTERS, PUBLIC

The leaves in autumn do not change color from the blighting touch of frost but from the process of natural decay. . . . And one of the great lessons the fall of the leaf teaches is this: Do your work well and then be ready to depart when God shall call.   ▶TRYON EDWARDS

AVARICE *See also:* LEVERAGED BUYOUTS

Poverty is in want of much, but avarice of everything.

▶PUBLIUS SYRUS

B

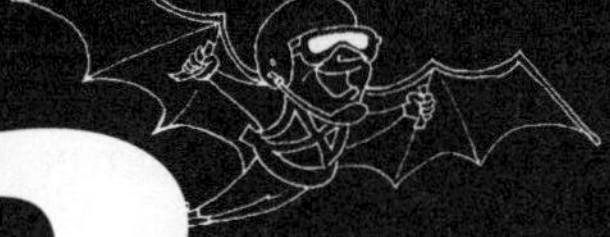

BABIES AND BABY BOOMERS *See also*: NANNYGATE, SESAME STREET and DEDUCTIONS, TAX

Of all vanities and fopperies, the vanity of high birth is the greatest. True nobility is derived from virtue, not from birth.

▶SIR RICHARD BURTON

BAD LUCK *See also*: SUPPORT SYSTEMS and FORTUNE COOKIES

Some souls are ennobled and elevated by seeming misfortunes, which then become blessings in disguise.   ▶EDWIN H. CHAPIN

BAG LADIES *See also*: ENTITLEMENTS and NATURAL LIVING

To struggle when hope is banished!
To live when life's salt is gone!
To dwell in a dream that's vanished!
To endure, and go calmly on!

▶ANONYMOUS

BALANCED BUDGETS *See also*: CONSTITUTIONAL AMENDMENTS

In a state, monetary gain is not to be considered as prosperity. Its prosperity will be found in righteousness.   ►CONFUCIUS

BALDNESS *See also*: COVER-UPS and SIMPLE LIFE, THE

There is more felicity on the far side of baldness than young men can possibly imagine.   ►LOGAN P. SMITH

BANKRUPTCY

The books are balanced in heaven, not here.   ►JOSH BILLINGS

BASEBALL

I am a great friend to public amusements, for they keep people from vice.   ►SAMUEL JOHNSON

BEAUTY

There's beauty all around our paths, if but our watchful eyes
Can trace it 'midst familiar things, and through their lowly guise.
►FELICIA HEMANS

BEGGARS *See also*: PENSIONS, PRESIDENTIAL AND CONGRESSIONAL

Better to be a living beggar than a buried emperor.

▶LA FONTAINE

BILLS *See also*: CREDIT AND CREDIT CARDS

Debt is the worst poverty.   ▶M. G. LICHTWER

BIRDS *See also*: CHICKEN SOUP

You cannot prevent the birds of sorrow from flying over your head, but you can prevent them from building nests in your hair.

▶CHINESE PROVERB

BLESSINGS *See also*: WORK ETHIC, THE

How blessings brighten as they take their flight.   ▶OWEN D. YOUNG

Heaven is blessed with perfect rest,
But the blessing of life is toil.

▶HENRY VAN DYKE

BLUSHING *See also*: RED INK

A blush is a sign that nature hangs out, to show where chastity and honor dwell. ▶CHRISTIAN SCRIVER

BODY BUILDING *See also*: LEAN AND MEAN

Rugged strength and radiant beauty—
These were one in Nature's plan;
Humble toil and heavenward duty—
These will form the perfect man.
▶SARAH J. HALE

BOTTOM LINES

For what is a man profited if he gain all the world, and lose his own soul? ▶MATTHEW 16:26

No man can tell whether he is rich or poor by turning to his ledger. It is the heart that makes a man rich. He is rich or poor according to what he is, not according to what he has. ▶HENRY WARD BEECHER

BOY WONDERS

Short is my date, but deathless my renown. ►HOMER

BRAVERY *See also*: DEDUCTIONS, TAX

Without a pause he draws his sword,
And thinks of country, not of reward.
►HOMER

BUDDHA'S EIGHTFOLD WAY TO ENLIGHTENMENT

Right view, right intention, right speech, right action, right livelihood, right effort, right mindfulness, right concentration.

BUSINESS AND BUSINESS CYCLES

Business underlies everything in our national life, including our spiritual life. ►PRESIDENT WOODROW WILSON

Business will be either better or worse. ►PRESIDENT CALVIN COOLIDGE

As the blessings of health and fortune have a beginning, so they must also find an end. Everything rises but to fall, and increases but to decay. ►SALLUST

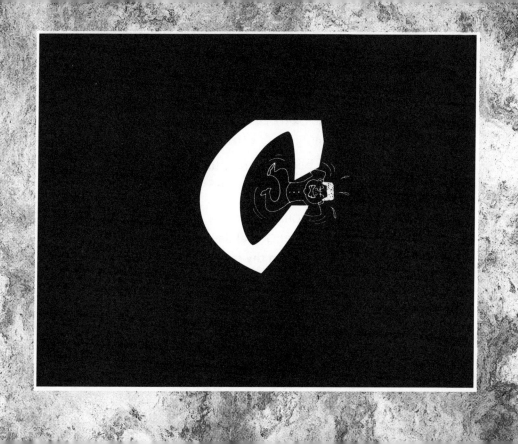

CABBAGES *See also*: EARLY RETIREMENT

Oh thrice and four times happy are those who plant cabbages.

▶RABELAIS

CALAMITIES *See also*: CORPORATE MERGERS

Calamity is the test of integrity.   ▶HENRY RICHARDSON

When any calamity has been suffered, the first thing to be remembered is, how much has been escaped.   ▶SAMUEL JOHNSON

CALIFORNIA *See also*: EARTHQUAKES

Blest power of sunshine! Genial day,
What balm, what life are in thy ray!

▶THOMAS MOORE

CALCULATORS

Count that day lost whose low descending sun
Views from thy hand no worthy action done.

▶ANONYMOUS

CAMPAIGN FUNDS See also: POLITICAL ACTION COMMITTEES and LOBBYISTS

Few men have virtue to withstand the highest bidder.

►President George Washington

CAMPAIGN PROMISES

He seemed for dignity composed and high exploit:
But all was false and hollow.

►Milton

CANNIBALS See also: EMPLOYERS

Man . . . is the most formidable of the beasts of prey, and, indeed, the only one that feeds systematically on its own species.

►William James

CAPITALISM AND COMMUNISM

Every form of government tends to perish by excess of its basic principle. ►Will Durant

Our little systems have their day. ►Alfred Lord Tennyson

CAREER LADDERS *See also*: NEPOTISM

If you wish to reach the highest, begin at the lowest. ▶SYRUS

Ambition often puts men upon doing the meanest offices, so climbing is performed in the same posture as creeping. ▶JONATHAN SWIFT

CASH AND CARRY

Of all the riches that we hug, of all the pleasure we enjoy, we can carry no more out of this world than out of a dream. ▶JAMES BONNELL

CATS *See also*: EXECUTIVE SUITES

Those who play with cats must expect to be scratched. ▶CERVANTES

CELEBRITY

Even dirt glitters when the sun is shining upon it. ▶GOETHE

CHANCE

All nature is but art unknown to thee.
All chance, direction, which thou canst not see.
▶ALEXANDER POPE

CHANGE *See also*: PROGRESS and DEATH

In this world of change, nought which comes stays, and nought which goes is lost. ▶MADAME SWETCHINE

CHARACTER AND CHARACTER ANALYSIS *See also*: COMPLEXES

You can tell a lot about a fellow's character by his way of eating jelly beans. ▶PRESIDENT RONALD REAGAN

The great hope of society is in individual character.
▶WILLIAM ELLERY CHANNING

The character that needs law to mend it is hardly worth the tinkering.
▶DOUGLAS JERROLD

CHARITY *See also*: DEDUCTIONS, TAX

Let shining Charity adorn your zeal,
'Tis the noblest impulse minds can feel.
▶AARON HILL

Nobody is ever impoverished through the giving of charity.
▶MAIMONIDES

CHICKEN SOUP See also: MOTHERS

The properties of the soul depend upon the condition of the body.

▶MAIMONIDES

God moves in a mysterious way
His cold cures to perform.

▶AFTER WILLIAM COWPER

CHIVALRY See also: SPIN DOCTORS

The age of chivalry is never past so long as there is a wrong left unredressed on earth. ▶CHARLES KINGSLEY

CHRISTMAS

A good conscience is a continual Christmas. ▶BEN FRANKLIN

I will honor Christmas in my heart and try to keep it all the year.

▶EBENEZER SCROOGE

CIVILITY

Civility costs nothing, and buys everything.

▶LADY MARY WORTLEY MONTAGUE

CIVILIZATION *See also*: MEDICAID

A decent provision for the poor is the true test of a civilization.

▶SAMUEL JOHNSON

CLASSES AND THE CLASS STRUGGLE

The common people and the highly placed have neither the same virtues nor the same vices. ▶LUC DE CLAPIER VAUVENARGUES

In war the strong make slaves of the weak, and in peace the rich make slaves of the poor. ▶OSCAR WILDE

You who have read the history of nations, from Moses down to the last election, where have you ever seen one class looking after the interests of another? ▶ELIZABETH C. STANTON

All the measures of goverment are directed to the purpose of making the rich richer and the poor poorer.

▶PRESIDENT WILLIAM HENRY HARRISON

CLOUDS *See also:* LUXURY and SUNSETS

My body is like a drifting cloud. I ask for nothing, I want nothing.

▶KAMO NO CHOMEI

CLOWNS *See also:* LITTLE THINGS THAT MEAN A LOT

By happy alchemy of mind,
They turn to pleasure all they find.

▶MATTHEW GREEN

COLLECTION AGENCIES

Often, it is not until a warrior loses both his chariot and his most valued horses that he realizes they were only a hindrance on his path to glory.   ▶VINITUS THE YOUNGER

COLLEGES *See also:* FINANCIAL AID

There is but one way to heaven for the learned and the unlearned.

▶JEREMY TAYLOR

The things taught in colleges and schools are not an education, but the means of an education.   ▶EMERSON

COMMUNICATION *See also*: INFORMATION SUPERHIGHWAYS

Forget not to do good and to communicate: for with such sacrifices God is well pleased.   ▶HEBREWS 13:16

COMPENSATION *See also*: GOLDEN PARACHUTES

No evil is without its compensation.   ▶SENECA

'Tis always morning somewhere in the world.   ▶R. H. HORNE

Since we are exposed to inevitable sorrows, wisdom is the art of finding compensation.   ▶PETER GASTON DE LÉVIS

COMPLEXES *See also*: REJECTION and MENTAL HEALTH

A man should not strive to eliminate his complexes but to get into harmony with them; they are what direct his conduct in the world.

▶FREUD

COMPUTERS *See also*: VIRUSES

Ease and speed in doing a thing do not give the work lasting solidity or exactness of beauty.   ▶PLUTARCH

CONCENTRATION

Depend upon it, sir, when a man knows he is to be hanged in a fortnight, it concentrates his mind wonderfully. ▶SAMUEL JOHNSON

CONFIDENCE *See also*: JOB INTERVIEWS

The human heart, at whatever age, opens only to the heart that opens in return. ▶MARIA EDGEWORTH

CONGRESS, U.S.

The virtues are lost in self-interest, as the rivers in the sea.
▶LA ROCHEFOUCAULD

Nonsense and noise will oft prevail, when honor and affection fail.
▶BISHOP WILLIAM LLOYD

CONSCIENCE *See also*: LAYOFFS

We never do wrong so thoroughly and so heartily as when we do it for conscience's sake. ►PASCAL

Never was the voice of conscience silenced without retribution.
►ANNA JAMESON

The laws of conscience, which we pretend to be derived from nature, proceed from custom. ►MONTAIGNE

CONSOLATION

The crash of the whole solar and stellar systems could only kill you once. ►CARLYLE

A consolation of being poor is that we are forced to deprive ourselves of the vices of the rich. ►ANONYMOUS

CONSTITUTIONAL AMENDMENTS

When the state is most corrupt, then the laws are most multiplied.
►TACITUS

CONTENTMENT

> Lord of himself, though not of lands;
> And having nothing, yet hath all.
>> ►Sir Henry Wotton

Whether happiness may come or not, one should try and prepare one's self to do without it.   ►George Eliot

CONVERSATION *See also*: LOAN COMPANIES

Our companions please us less from the charms we find in their conversation than from those they find in ours.   ►Lord Brooke Greville

CORPORATIONS

You never expected justice from a corporation, did you? They have neither a soul to lose nor a body to kick.   ►Lord Thurlow

I have always believed that the first business corporation was conceived by a band of pirates who had tired of living at sea.
>> ►Sir Trevor Buke

CORPORATIONS, ANNUAL REPORTS OF

There is in us more of the appearance of sense and virtue than of the reality. ▶MARGUERITE DE VALOIS

Get your facts first, and you can distort 'em as you will.
▶MARK TWAIN

CORPORATE MERGERS *See also*: SYNERGY and LAYOFFS

Nothing in the world is single,
All things by a law divine
In one spirit meet and mingle.
▶SHELLEY

CORPORATE TAKEOVERS AND TAKEBACKS

Fishes live in the sea as men do on land. The great ones eat up the little ones. ▶SHAKESPEARE

COST OF LIVING, THE

Money is not required to buy one necessity of the soul. ▶THOREAU

COURAGE

Fate can take away riches, but not courage. ▶SENECA

It were no virtue to bear calamities if we did not feel them.
▶MADAME NECKER

We cannot conquer fate and necessity, yet we can yield to them in such a manner as to be greater than if we could.
▶WALTER SAVAGE LANDOR

COURTESY See also: PUBLIC RELATIONS. Do not see: LAYOFFS

When my friends are blind of one eye, I look at them in profile.
▶JOSEPH JOUBERT

Small courtesies sweeten life; great ones ennoble it.
▶CHRISTIAN N. BOVEE

COURTSHIP

Courtship consists in a number of quiet attentions, not so pointed as to alarm, nor so vague as to be misunderstood. ▶LAURENCE STERNE

COVER-UPS *See also*: SAVINGS AND LOAN SCANDALS, IRAN-CONTRA, and WHITEWATER

He that has no real esteem for any of the virtues can best assume the appearance of them all. ►CALEB COLTON

There is nothing more contemptible than a bald man who pretends to have hair. ►MARTIAL

CREDIT AND CREDIT CARDS *See also*: DEBT

Fine manners are like personal beauty—a letter of credit everywhere. ►CYRUS A. BARTOL

Creditors have better memories than debtors. ►BEN FRANKLIN

Money often costs too much, and power and pleasure are not cheap.
►EMERSON

CREDULITY *See also*: MUTUAL FUNDS

It is as wise to moderate our beliefs as our desires.
►WALTER SAVAGE LANDOR

We believe easily what we fear or what we desire. ►LA FONTAINE

CRIME *See also*: SPIN DOCTORS

Most crimes are sanctioned in some form or other when they take grand names. ►OUIDA

CRITICS

Those who have no wit are prone to doubt that of others.

►LADY MARGUERITE BLESSINGTON

CRUELTY *See also*: LEAN AND MEAN

Cruelty, like every other vice, requires no motives outside of itself; it only requires opportunity.   ►GEORGE ELIOT

CULTURE

Great culture is often betokened by great simplicity.
►MADAME DOROTHÉ DELUZY

Man is born barbarous, and is ransomed from the condition of beasts only by being cultivated.   ►ALPHONSE DE LAMARTINE

I am very sure that any man of common understanding may, by culture, care, attention and labor, make himself whatever he pleases, except a great poet.   ►LORD CHESTERFIELD

CURIOSITY *See also*: GNUS

Curiosity is one of the permanent and certain characteristics of a vigorous mind.   ►SAMUEL JOHNSON

CUSTOM

Custom is often only the antiquity of error. ▶Cyprian

We wouldn't dream of living in the dwellings of our ancestors the cavemen, but some of their social and political customs are still popular in our homes, workplaces, and seats of government.

> ▶Harriet Sayres

CYBERSPACE See also: virtual reality

It is not worthwhile to go round the world to count the cats in Zanzibar. ▶Thoreau

CYNICISM

No matter how cynical you get , it's hard to keep up. ▶Lily Tomlin

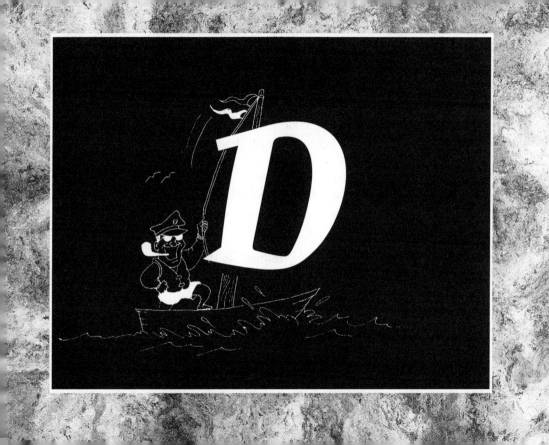

DANCING

Let your life lightly dance on the edges of time like dew on the tip of a leaf. ▶Rabindranath Tagore

DATA BASES *See also*: COMPUTERS

Many shall run to and fro, and knowledge shall be increased.
▶Daniel 12:4

DATING GAME, THE *See also*: CONVERSATION

Contact with a high-minded woman is good for the life of any man.
▶Henry Vincent

Romance has been elegantly defined as the offspring of fiction and love. ▶Benjamin Disraeli

Magnificent promises are always to be suspected.
▶Theodore Parker

The pursuit, even of the best things, ought to be calm and tranquil.
▶Cicero

DAYS OF OUR YEARS, THE

Days are scrolls; write on them only what you want remembered.
▶BACHYA IBN PAKUDA

DEATH *See also*: EQUAL OPPORTUNITY

Remember, not one penny can we take with us into the unknown land. ▶SENECA

Pale death enters with impartial step the cottages of the poor and the palaces of the rich. ▶HORACE

Say not good night, but in some brighter clime, bid me good morning. ▶ANNA LETITIA BARBAULD

God's finger touched him, and he slept. ▶ALFRED LORD TENNYSON

DEBT *See also*: CREDIT

It is always pleasant to be generous though very vexatious to pay debts. ▶EMERSON

DECEIT *See also*: SOCIAL CONTRACT, THE

Deceit is the false road to happiness. And all the joys we travel through to vice, like fairy banquets, vanish when we touch them.

► AARON HILL

DEDICATION

The greater the difficulty, the more glory in surmounting it. Skillful pilots gain their reputation from storms and tempests. ► EPICURUS

DEDUCTIONS, TAX *See also*: PATRIOTISM

Whenever our country calls, we should yield our treasure up, nor own to a sense beyond the public safety. ► HENRY BROOKE

DEEDS *See also*: WORK ETHIC, THE

Our deeds are seeds of fate, sown here on earth, but bringing forth their harvest in eternity. ► GEORGE DANA BOARDMAN

DEFEAT *See also*: LAYOFFS

Defeat should never be a source of discouragement, but rather a fresh stimulus. ► ROBERT SOUTH

DEFECTS

In the intercourse of life, we often please more by our defects than by our good qualities. ▶La Rochefoucauld

DEFERENCE *See also*: UNEMPLOYMENT OFFICES

Deference is the most complicated, the most indirect, the most elegant of all compliments. ▶William Shenstone

DEPORTMENT

What's a fine person, or a beauteous face,
Unless deportment gives them decent grace?
▶Charles Churchill

DEPRESSION *See also*: PROZAC

We degrade life by our follies and vices, and then complain that the unhappiness which is only their accompaniment is inherent in the constitution of things. ▶Christian N. Bovee

Employment and hardships prevent melancholy. ▶Samuel Johnson

DESIRE *See also*: LUXURY

What we desire in youth comes to haunt us in maturity.

▶HILDA HOWARD

DIETS

Hope is a light diet, but very stimulating.   ▶BALZAC

Better is a dinner of herbs where love is, than a stalled ox and hatred therewith.   ▶PROVERBS 15:17

DIGNITY *See also*: SELF-HELP BOOKS

Dignity consists not in possessing honors, but in the consciousness that we deserve them.   ▶ARISTOTLE

DISASTERS *See also*: EXPECTATIONS, DIMINISHED

Looking back, we shall see that what we desired would have been fatal to us, and what we would have avoided was essential.

▶FRANÇOIS DE FÉNELON

DISCRIMINATION *See also*: SESAME STREET and MISS PIGGY

It's not easy being green.   ►KERMIT THE FROG

DISGRACE

The man who dies rich dies disgraced.   ►ANDREW CARNEGIE

DIVORCE *See also*: BANKRUPTCY

One last, long sigh to love and thee, then back to busy life again.
►BYRON

Sometimes a noble failure serves the world as faithfully as a distinguished success.   ►EDWARD DOWDEN

DOGMAS *See also*: THINK TANKS

Everyone clings to the doctrine he has happened upon, as to a rock against which he has been thrown by a tempest.   ►CICERO

DOGS *See also*: CATS

> Master, go on, and I will follow thee
> To the last gasp, with truth and loyalty.
>> ►SHAKESPEARE

DOORS *See also*: WINDOWS OF OPPORTUNITY

> God enters by a private door into every individual.   ►EMERSON

> The soul selects its own Society—
> Then shuts the door.
>> ►EMILY DICKINSON

DOUBT *See also*: SELF-RESPECT

> Beware of doubt—faith is the subtle chain
> Which binds us to the infinite: the voice
> Of a deep life within, that will remain
> Until we crowd it thence.
>> ►ELIZABETH OAKES SMITH

DOWNSIZING *See also*: LESS IS MORE

Like the dainty bees who prepare the honey for our mead and holiday cakes, small service is often the truest and sweetest gift to mankind. ►F. CAVENDISH

DRAWING ROOMS *See also*: HOMELESSNESS

Disorder in a drawing room is vulgar. ►JOHN RUSKIN

DREAMS

Life is a dream and death an awakening. ►LAURENT DE LA BEAUMELLE

I have a dream that my four children will one day live in a nation where they will not be judged by the color of their skin, but by the content of their character. ►MARTIN LUTHER KING, JR.

DROWNING *See also*: YACHTS

Don't give up hoping when the ship goes down,
Grab a spar or something—just refuse to drown.
►LOUIS E. THAYER

DRUNKENNESS *See also*: WATER

Greatness of any kind has no greater foe than the habit of drinking.

►SIR WALTER SCOTT

DUTY *See also*: PENSIONS, PRESIDENTIAL

Then on! then on! where duty leads,

My course be onward still.

►BISHOP REGINALD HEBER

Our duty is to be useful, not according to our desires but according to our powers. ►HENRI AMIEL

EARLY RETIREMENT *See also*: CORPORATE TAKEOVERS

Obedience and resignation are our personal offerings upon the altar of duty. ▶HOSEA BALLOU

EARNESTNESS *See also*: SAVINGS AND LOAN SCANDALS

A man in earnest finds means, or if he cannot find them, he creates them. ▶WILLIAM E. CHANNING

EARTHQUAKES *See also*: BUSINESS CYCLES

Where there is rejoicing, there shall also be trembling. ▶THE TALMUD

ECONOMICS

There is seldom anything new under the sun in economic policy, where the allegedly new generally turns out to be the discard of a previous century in flimsy disguise. ▶MILTON FRIEDMAN

ECONOMIC RECOVERY *See also*: PRIVATE SECTOR, THE and SERVICE INDUSTRIES

To know how to wait is the great secret of success. ▶JOSEPH DE MAISTRE

Never despair; but if you do, work on in despair. ▶EDMUND BURKE

ECONOMICS, TRICKLE-DOWN

Remember that every drop of rain that falls bears into the bosom of the earth a quality of beautiful fertility. ▸G. H. LEWES

EDITORIAL WRITERS

He is wise who can instruct us and assist us in the business of daily virtuous living. ▸THOMAS CARLYLE

EDUCATION *See also*: JOB RETRAINING and FINANCIAL AID

The best and most important of every man's education is that which he gives himself. ▸EDWARD GIBBON

No inheritance can supply the want of a virtuous education.
▸THOMAS WILSON

The wisest man can always learn something from the humblest peasant. ▸JEAN ANTOINE PETIT-SENN

The best education in the world is that got by struggling to get a living. ▸WENDELL PHILLIPS

EFFICIENCY *See also*: NORTH AMERICAN FREE TRADE AGREEMENT and UNEMPLOYMENT

The more complete the despotism, the more smoothly all things move on the surface. ►ELIZABETH C. STANTON

An efficiency at billiards is a sure sign of a misspent youth.

►BENJAMIN DISRAELI

ELECTIONS AND ELECTION CAMPAIGNS

See, the conquering hero comes!

Sound the trumpet, beat the drums!

►THOMAS MORELL

Life often presents us with a choice of evils rather than of good.

►CALEB C. COLTON

Trust not too much to an enchanting face. ►VIRGIL

Our hands have met, but not our hearts. ►THOMAS HOOD

Magnificent promises are always to be suspected. ►THEODORE PARKER

Nothing good ever comes of violence. ►MARTIN LUTHER

EMPLOYERS *See also*: JOB INTERVIEWS

In civilized society there is found a race of men who retain the instincts of the aboriginal cannibal and live upon their fellow men as a natural food. ►E. G. BULWER-LYTTON

ENDS AND MEANS

So act as to treat everyone as an end and someone of value, and never only as a means to something more important. ►KANT

ENTERTAINMENT

Be not forgetful to entertain strangers, for thereby some have entertained angels unawares. ►HEBREWS 13:2

ENTITLEMENTS *See also*: UNEMPLOYMENT INSURANCE and PENSIONS, PRESIDENTIAL AND CONGRESSSIONAL

And so, my fellow Americans, ask not what your country can do for you—ask what you can do for your country.

►PRESIDENT JOHN F. KENNEDY

EQUAL OPPORTUNITY *See also*: OLD BOY NETWORKS

The law, in its majestic equality, forbids the rich as well as the poor to sleep under bridges, to beg in the streets, and to steal bread.

▶ANATOLE FRANCE

EQUALITY

Of course I believe in equality, but I like to choose the people I'm going to be equal to. ▶FRANCIS STUYVESANT

Disease generally begins that equality which death completes; the distinctions which set one man so much above another are very little perceived in the gloom of a sick-chamber. ▶SAMUEL JOHNSON

ESTATES *See also*: SIMPLE LIFE, THE

The care of a large estate is an unpleasant thing.   ▶JUVENAL

ETERNITY

Nothing is eternal but that which is done for God and others. That which is done for self dies.   ▶AUGHEY

The thought of eternity consoles us for the shortness of life.
▶CHRÉTIEN MALESHERBES

Let me dream that love goes with us to the shore unknown.
▶FELICIA HEMANS

ETIQUETTE

Fine manners need the support of fine manners in others.
▶EMERSON

Be to her virtues very kind;
Be to her faults a little blind.
▶MATTHEW PRIOR

Serenity of manners is the zenith of beauty.   ▶F. BREMER

EVICTIONS *See also*: HOMELESSNESS

Nature alone is permanent. ►LONGFELLOW

Go forth under the open sky, and list to nature's teaching.
►WILLIAM CULLEN BRYANT

EVIL

Seek for good, but expect evil. ►CERVANTES

When choosing between two evils, I always like to take the one I haven't tried before. ►MAE WEST

EXECUTIVES AND EXECUTIVE PERKS *See also*: OPULENCE

Executive ability is deciding quickly and getting somebody else to do the work. ►J. G. POLLARD

EXECUTIVES, REDUNDANT *See also*: GOLDEN PARACHUTES

To bear injuries, or annoying or vexatious events, meekly, patiently, prayerfully, and with self-control, is more praiseworthy than the taking of a city. ►CHARLES SIMMONS

EXECUTIVE SUITES *See also*: GLASS CEILINGS

Distinction of rank is necessary for the economy of the world, and was never called in question but by barbarians and enthusiasts.

▶NICHOLAS ROWE

Tyrants are seldom free; the cares and the instruments of their tyranny enslave them. ▶GEORGE SANTAYANA

EXERCISE *See also*: MOUNTAIN CLIMBING

The only way for a rich man to be healthy is by exercise and abstinence, to live as if he was poor. ►SIR WILLIAM TEMPLE

EXPECTATIONS, DIMINISHED

It is expectation makes a blessing dear; heaven were not heaven if we knew what it were. ►JOHN SUCKLING

If you can't catch a bird of paradise, better take a wet hen.
►NIKITA KHRUSHCHEV

FAILURE

A first failure is often a blessing.　▶A. L. Brown

In great attempts it is glorious even to fail.　▶Longinus

The only failure a man ought to fear is failure in cleaving to the purpose he has in mind.　▶George Eliot

FAIRIES AND FAIRYLAND　*See also*: SYNERGY

Be secret and discreet; the fairy favors are lost when not concealed.
▶John Dryden

Wherever is love and loyalty, great purposes and lofty souls, even though in a hovel or a mine, there is fairyland.　▶Charles Kingsley

FAIRY TALES

The soul without imagination is what an observatory would be without a telescope.　▶Henry Ward Beecher

Everyone's life is a fairy tale written by God's fingers.
▶Hans Christian Andersen

FAITH

Faith. You can do very little with it, but you can do nothing without it.
▶SAMUEL BUTLER

If there is a faith that can move mountains, it is faith in your own power. ▶MARIE E. VON ESCHENBACH

How many things that served us yesterday as articles of faith are fables for us today. ▶MONTAIGNE

FAMILIES AND FAMILY VALUES *See also*: CHICKEN SOUP

Hail, wedded love, mysterious law, true source of human offspring!
▶MILTON

A happy family is but an earlier heaven. ▶SIR JOHN BOWRING

A happy union with wife and child is like the music of lutes and harps. ▶CONFUCIUS

The spirit and tone of your home will have great influence on your children. If it is what it ought to be, it will fasten conviction on their minds, however wicked they may become. ▶RICHARD CECIL

FASHION

The fashion of this world passeth away. ▶I CORINTHIANS

Every generation laughs at the old fashions, but follows religiously the new. ▶THOREAU

FAST TRACK, THE *See also*: CAREER LADDERS and NEPOTISM

> Oh, sons of earth! attempt ye still to rise,
> By mountain piled on mountain to the skies?
> Heav'n still with laughter the toil surveys,
> And buries madmen in the heaps they raise.
>
> ▶ALEXANDER POPE

FEAR

There is great beauty in going through life fearlessly. Half our fears are baseless, the other half discreditable. ▶CHRISTIAN N. BOVEE

FIDELITY *See also*: FAMILY VALUES

All beauties are to be honored, but only one embraced.

▶GEORGE SANTAYANA

FINANCIAL ADVISERS

Saying is one thing, and doing is another. ►MONTAIGNE

FINANCIAL AID

Who will not support a scholar will see no blessing.

►ELEAZAR BEN PEDAT

Great is the reward for hospitality to a scholar. ►ELIEZER BEN JOSE

FIRST LADIES *See also*: WHITEWATER

There is a woman at the beginning of all great things.

►ALPHONSE DE LAMARTINE

It is difficult for a woman to be anything good when she is not believed in. ►GEORGE ELIOT

FISHING *See also*: WANT ADS

Let your hook always be cast. In a pool where you least expect it, there will be a fish. ►OVID

FLATTERY *See also:* JOB INTERVIEWS

Just praise is only a debt, but flattery is a present. ▶SAMUEL JOHNSON

Flattery, if judiciously administered, is always acceptable, however much we may despise the flatterer. ▶LADY BLESSINGTON

FLIRTING

As the rolling stone gathers no moss, so the roving heart gathers no affections. ▶ANNA JAMESON

FOOD *See also:* MCDONALD'S

If a man has nothing to eat, fasting is the most intelligent thing he can do. ▶HERMANN HESSE

The chief pleasure in eating does not consist in costly seasoning, or exquisite flavor, but in yourself. ▶HORACE

FOOD STAMPS *See also:* ENTITLEMENTS. *Do not see:* GOLDEN PARACHUTES

A crust eaten in peace is better than a banquet partaken in anxiety.

▶AESOP

FOOTBALL

The exercise of all the muscles of the body in their due proportion is one great secret of health and comfort as well as of strength, and the full development of manly vigor.　▶WILLIAM HALL

FORTUNE COOKIES

We do not know what is good or bad fortune.　▶ROUSSEAU

Much wisdom often goes with fewest words.　▶SOPHOCLES

FOUND INSIDE FORTUNE COOKIES IN BROOKLYN

You will be successful in love.　▶SHANGHAI VILLA

You will be unusually successful in business.　▶SHANG-CHAI KOSHER

Meeting adversity well is the source of your strength.
　　　▶RICHARD YEE RESTAURANT

No one knows what he can do till he tries.
　　　▶MR. TANG OF NOSTRAND AVENUE

The star of riches is shining upon you.　▶HOUSE OF WING WAH

FREEBIES *See also*: PENSIONS, PRESIDENTIAL AND CONGRESSIONAL

Gifts come from above in their own peculiar form. ▶GOETHE

FREEDOM

He who desires naught will always be free. ▶LEFEBVRE-LABOULAYE

No man is free who cannot control himself. ▶PYTHAGORAS

Thank God for poverty that makes and keeps us free, and lets us go our unobstrusive way, glad of the sun and rain, upright, serene, humane, contented with the fortunes of the day. ▶BLISS CARMAN

FREE LUNCH

A country in which there is no free lunch is no longer a free country.

▶ARTHUR "BUGS" BAER

FRIENDS AND FRIENDSHIP Do *not* see: EMPLOYERS

Of friends, however humble, scorn not one. ▶WORDSWORTH

A book is a friend that never deceives. ▶DE PIXÉRÉCOURT

It is good to have friends at court. ▶CHARLES LAMB

If a man does not make new acquaintances as he advances through life, he will soon find himself left alone. A man, sir, should keep his friendships in a constant repair. ▶SAMUEL JOHNSON

FRUSTRATION

We mount to heaven mostly on the ruins of our cherished schemes, finding our failures were successes. ▶A. B. ALCOTT

FUEL BILLS

If winter comes, can spring be far behind? ▶SHELLEY

FURNITURE See also: REPOSSESSION

I would rather sit on a pumpkin and have it all to myself than to be crowded on a velvet cushion. ▶THOREAU

FUTURE, THE

The veil which covers the face of futurity is woven by the hand of mercy. ▸E. G. BULWER-LYTTON

Cease to inquire what the future has in store. Take as a gift whatever the day brings forth. ▸HORACE

Events of all sorts creep or fly exactly as God pleases.
▸WILLIAM COWPER

I never think of the future. It comes soon enough. ▸ALBERT EINSTEIN

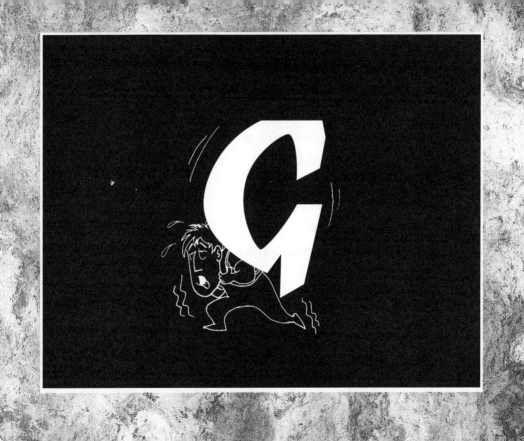

GAMBLING

It may be that the race is not always to the swift, nor to the strong—but that's the way to bet. ▶DAMON RUNYON

GAME PLANS *See also*: JUNK BONDS

Human foresight often leaves its proudest possessor only a choice of evils. ▶CALEB C. COLTON

GARDENING *See also*: JOB RETRAINING

Sow good services, and sweet remembrances will grow from them.
▶MADAME DE STAËL

To cultivate a garden is to walk with God. ▶CHRISTIAN N. BOVEE

GENERATION GAPS

The wisdom of one generation is the stupidity of the next, but it may be the other way around. ▶ALEX UNTERVILLE

How soon men and events are forgotten. Each generation lives in another world. ▶ANONYMOUS

GENES

Everyone is as God made him, and often a great deal worse.

▶Cervantes

GENIUS

Poverty is the stepmother of genius. ▶H. W. Shaw

GINGRICH, NEWT

Ring in the nobler modes of life,
With sweeter manners, purer laws.

▶Alfred Lord Tennyson

GIVE-AND-TAKE

In your relations with people it is necessary to try to give them as much as possible and to take from them as little as possible.

▶Tolstoy

Give according to your means, or God will make your means according to your giving. ▶John Hall

GLASS CEILINGS See also: PRIVATE CLUBS

> Learn from Icarus not to soar too high,
> The sun is and will be Lord in the sky.
>
> ►CHARLES PROCTOR

A thing of beauty is a joy forever, especially if she never nags for a raise or promotion.   ►NORMA JACOBSON

GLOBAL ECONOMY

> For I dipped into the future, far as human eye could see,
> Saw the vision of the world, and all the wonder that would be;
> Saw the heavens fill with commerce, argosies of magic sails,
> Pilots of the purple twilight, dropping down with costly bales.
>
> ►TENNYSON

GLUTTONY See also: SOUP KITCHENS, FREE

When I behold a fashionable table set out in all its magnificence, I fancy that I see gout and dropsies, fevers and lethargies, with other innumerable distempers lying in ambush among the dishes.   ►ADDISON

GNUS *See also*: INFORMATION SUPERHIGHWAYS

The gnu is extremely curious. He climbs to the top of anthills for objects he can be curious about. He will risk his life to find out what is what. This is seldom worth finding out but the gnu doesn't mind.

▶WILL CUPPY

GOD

God shows his contempt of wealth by the kind of person He selected to receive it. ▶AUSTIN O'MALLEY

The perfect love of God knows no difference between the poor and the rich. ▶PACUVIUS

There is no religion without mystery. God Himself is the great secret of Nature. ▶CHATEAUBRIAND

GOLD

A good heart is worth gold. ▶SHAKESPEARE

GOLDEN PARACHUTES

Christmas won't be Christmas without any presents.
►Louisa May Alcott

The gods see the deeds of the righteous.   ►Ovid

It is better to be nobly remembered than nobly born.   ►John Ruskin

GOLDEN RULE, THE

Therefore all things whatsoever ye would that men should do to you, do ye even so to them, for this is the law and the prophets.
►Matthew 7:12

GOLF

The real test in golf and in life is not in keeping out of the rough, but in getting out after we are in.   ►John H. Moore

GOOD-BYE See also: LAYOFFS

Could we see when and where we are to meet again, we would be more tender when we bid our friends good-bye.   ►Ouida

GOOD CHEER *See also:* PROZAC

They are sending me to the scaffold. Well, my friends, we must go to it gaily. ▶DANTON

I have gout, asthma, and seven other maladies, but am otherwise very well. ▶SYDNEY SMITH

I have often thought of death, and I find it the least of all evils.
▶JEREMY TAYLOR

GOOD VISION

We only see clearly when we have reached the depths of woe. ▶Ouida

GOVERNMENT AND GOVERNMENT OFFICIALS *See also*: SAVINGS AND LOAN SCANDALS

Every nation has the government it deserves. ▶Joseph de Maistre

Government, like dress, is the badge of lost innocence.
▶Thomas Paine

The crimes of citizens are the virtues of their government.
▶St. Cyprian

In a change of government, the poor seldom change anything except their master. ▶Phaedrus

Government is an association of men who do violence to the rest of us. ▶Tolstoy

The object of government is the welfare of the people. The material progress and prosperity of a nation are desirable chiefly so far as they lead to the moral and material welfare of all good citizens.
▶President Theodore Roosevelt

GRAVES *See also*: COVER-UPS

Gilded graves do worms unfold.　▶SHAKESPEARE

The earth opens impartially her bosom to receive the beggar and the prince.　▶HORACE

The grave is a very small hillock, but we can see farther from it, when standing on it, than from the highest mountain in the world.

▶A. THOLUCK

GREATNESS

Great men are never sufficiently shown but in struggles.

▶EDMUND BURKE

That man is great who rises to the emergencies of the occasion, and becomes master of the situation.　▶DONN PIATT

GREED *See also*: HARVARD BUSINESS SCHOOL

The lust of gold, unfeeling and remorseless, is the last corruption of degenerate man.　▶SAMUEL JOHNSON

GRIEF *See also*: SMILIN' THROUGH

No grief is so acute but time ameliorates it.   ▶CICERO

No grief reaches the dead.   ▶SALLUST

Happiness is beneficial for the body, but it is grief that develops the power of the mind.   ▶PROUST

GUILT *See also*: LANDLORDS

Guilt, though it may attain temporal splendor, can never confer real happiness. . . while the paths of virtue, though seldom those of worldly greatness, are always those of pleasantness and peace.

▶SIR WALTER SCOTT

GURUS *See also*: TALK SHOWS AND TALK SHOW HOSTS

He who knows does not speak.

He who speaks does not know.

▶LAO-TSE

HABITS

We are drawn toward a thing because we believe it is good. We end by being chained to it because it has become a necessity.
▶SIMONE WEIL

The long habit of living indisposeth us for dying. ▶SIR THOMAS BROWNE

HANDICAPS *See also:* PROGRESS

The growth of computer power and microelectronics will lead to a burst of hope and opportunity for Americans who are handicapped or disabled. ▶NEWT GINGRICH

HAPPINESS

It is wrong to assume that men of great wealth are always happy.
▶JOHN D. ROCKEFELLER

Our happiness in this world depends on the affections which we are enabled to inspire. ▶DUCHESSE DE PRASLIN

Happiness grows at our own fireside, and is not to be picked in strangers' gardens. ▶DOUGLAS JERROLD

HAPPY THOUGHTS

> The world is so full of a number of things,
> I'm sure we should all be as happy as kings.
>
> ►ROBERT LOUIS STEVENSON

He that is down can fall no lower.　►SAMUEL BUTLER

He that dies pays all debts.　►SHAKESPEARE

HARVARD BUSINESS SCHOOL

The worst education, which teaches self-denial, is better than the best education which teaches everything else and not that.

►JOHN STERLING.

HATS

Live your life, do your work, then take your hat. ▶THOREAU

HEALTH See also: HEALTH PLAN, NATIONAL and MAJOR MEDICAL

Refuse to be ill. Never tell people you are ill; never own it to yourself. Illness is one of those things which a man should resist on principle at the onset. ▶E. G. BULWER-LYTTON

Earth has no sorrow that heaven cannot heal. ▶THOMAS MOORE

By medicine life may be prolonged; yet death will seize the doctor too. ▶SHAKESPEARE

Be sober and temperate, and you will be healthy. ▶BEN FRANKLIN

Health and cheerfulness mutually beget each other. ▶JOSEPH ADDISON

Health is the second blessing that we mortals are capable of; a blessing that money cannot buy. ▶IZAAK WALTON

HEALTH INSURANCE

Often in human affairs the simplest ends can be achieved only by the most roundabout and most outlandish means. ▶ERIC HOFFER

HEALTH PLAN, NATIONAL

> For of all sad words of tongue or pen,
> The saddest are these: "It might have been."
>> ►WHITTIER

Go north, young family!   ►ANONYMOUS

HEARTS AND HEART DISEASE

The heart that has once been bathed in love's pure fountain retains the pulse of youth forever.   ►WALTER SAVAGE LANDOR

Nothing is too late till the tired heart shall cease to palpitate.
>> ►LONGFELLOW

HEAVEN *See also*: RETIREMENT

As much of heaven is visible as we have eyes to see.   ►WILLIAM WINTER

There are glimpses of heaven to us in every act, or thought, or word, that raises us above ourselves.   ►A. P. STANLEY

Heaven will not be heaven if I do not meet my wife there.
>> ►PRESIDENT ANDREW JACKSON

HELL

The pride of dying rich raises the loudest laugh in hell.   ▶John Foster

The mind is its own place, and in itself can make a heaven of hell, a hell of heaven.   ▶Milton

HEROISM See also: POVERTY

There is more heroism in self-denial than in deeds of arms.   ▶Seneca

Prodigious actions may as well be done
By weaver's issue as by prince's son.

▶John Dryden

HOMES AND HOUSING See also: LANDLORDS and FAMILY VALUES

Our home is still home, be it ever so homely.   ▶Charles Dibdin

Every one in his own house and God in all of them.   ▶Cervantes

He is happiest, be he king or peasant, who finds peace in his home.
▶Goethe

A happy home is the single spot of rest which a man has upon this earth for the cultivation of his noblest sensibilities.   ▶F. W. Robertson

HOMELESSNESS *See also:* MANSIONS and SHELTERS, PUBLIC

You cannot breathe too much of the open air. ▶DR. JOHN ABERNETHY

Oh, what a glory doth this world put on for him who, with a fervent heart, goes forth under the bright and glorious sky! ▶LONGFELLOW

HONESTY

A grain of honesty and native worth is of more value than all the adventitious ornaments, estates, or preferments. ▶LORD SHAFTESBURY

For the merchant, even honesty is a financial speculation.
▶CHARLES BAUDELAIRE

HOPE

Nothing happens in life either as it is feared or as it is hoped.
▶Jean B. A. Karr

The hope of all earnest souls must be realized.   ▶Whittier

> Hope, like the gleaming taper's light,
> Adorns and cheers our way;
> And still, as darker grows the night,
> Emits a brighter ray.
> ▶Oliver Goldsmith

Hope, deceitful as she is, serves at least to conduct us through life by an agreeable path.   ▶La Rochefoucauld

Hope is a workingman's dream.   ▶Pliny

HOSPITALITY

Like many other virtues, hospitality is practiced in its perfection by the poor. If the rich did their share, how the woes of this world would be lightened!   ▶Mrs. C. M. Kirkland

HUD SCANDALS *See also:* SAVINGS AND LOAN SCANDAL

Heaven never helps the man who will not help himself. ►SOPHOCLES

A conservative government is an organized conspiracy.
►BENJAMIN DISRAELI

HULA HOOPS *See also:* SPIN DOCTORS

He that will make a good use of any part of his life must allow a large part of it to recreation. ►JOHN LOCKE

HUMAN NATURE

To forget that man is a fantastic creature is to ignore his most crucial trait, and when contemplating human nature the wildest guesses and hunches are legitimate. ►UNKNOWN

When man is not properly trained, he is the most savage animal on the face of the earth. ►PLATO

HUMILITY

Don't aim to be an earthly Saint, with eyes fixed on a star,
Just try to be the fellow that your Mother thinks you are.
►WILL S. ADKIN

HUMOR

A difference of taste in jokes is a great strain on the affections.
►GEORGE ELIOT

HUNGER

Hunger is the teacher of the arts, and the bestower of invention.
►PERSIUS

They are as sick who surfeit with too much as they that starve with
nothing. ►SHAKESPEARE

IDEAS *See also*: CAPITALISM AND COMMUNISM and RELIGION

An idea isn't responsible for the people who believe in it.

▶DON MARQUIS

IDEALS

It is better for men, it is better for women, that each somewhat idealize the other. Much is lost when life has lost its atmosphere and is reduced to naked fact. ▶GAIL HAMILTON

IDENTITY AND IDENTITY CRISES

The greatest thing in the world is for a man to know how to be himself. ▶MONTAIGNE

Oh! It is great to shake off the trammels of the world and of public opinion—to lose our importunate, tormenting, everlasting identity and become the creature of the moment, clear of all ties.

▶WILLIAM HAZLITT

I'm nobody, Who are you?
Are you—Nobody—too?

▶EMILY DICKINSON

IMAGINATION

Were it not for imagination, Sir, a man would be as happy in the arms of a chambermaid as of a duchess. ▶SAMUEL JOHNSON

A ray of imagination or of wisdom may enlighten the universe, and flow into remotest centuries. ▶BISHOP GEORGE BERKELEY

Imagination disposes of everything; it creates beauty, justice, and happiness, which is everything in the world. ▶PASCAL

IMMORTALITY *See also*: PUBLIC RELATIONS

All men's souls are immortal, but the souls of the righteous are both immortal and divine. ▶SOCRATES

IMPOSSIBLE, THE

Don't tell me anything is impossible. Let's try it first. ▶JOSEPH PAPP

INDEPENDENCE

He who is lord of himself, and exists upon his own resources, is a noble but a rare being. ▶SIR E. BRYDGES

INFLATION

Prefer loss of money to the wealth of dishonest gain; the former vexes you for a time, but the latter will bring you lasting remorse. ▶CHILO

INFORMATION SUPERHIGHWAYS *See also*: MEDIA CONGLOMERATES

It is not so important to know everything as to know the exact value of everything, to appreciate what we learn, and to arrange what we know. ▶HANNAH MORE

Knowledge is but folly unless it is guided by grace. ▶GEORGE HERBERT

INHERITANCE

Beware of inherited wealth. ▶ROBERT R. YOUNG

INTELLECTUALS *See also*: THINK TANKS

In almost every civilization we know of, the intellectuals have been either allied with those in power or members of a governing elite, and consequently indifferent to the fate of the masses. ▶ERIC HOFFER

INTELLIGENCE

The sky is full of tokens that speak to the intelligent. ▶HUGH MILLER

INTEREST GROUPS

The interest of the state is in intimate connection with those of the rich individuals belonging to it. ▶ALEXANDER HAMILTON

INTEREST RATES

> For each ecstatic instant
> We must an anguish pay
> In keen and quivering ratio
> To the ecstacy.
>
> ▶EMILY DICKINSON

INTERPERSONAL RELATIONS *See also:* GLASS CEILINGS

During an encounter with a man who is trying to intimidate me with his power or position in society, I try to imagine him with his trousers down and sitting on a potty. ▶W. SOMERSET MAUGHAM

INTRODUCTIONS

Adversity introduces a man to himself. ▶ANONYMOUS

INVESTMENTS

Goodness is the only investment that never fails. ▶THOREAU

IRAN-CONTRA INQUIRY

If God should punish men according to what they deserve, He would not leave on the back of the earth so much as a beast. ▶THE KORAN

No one is ever made better by someone telling him how rotten he is; but many are made better by avowing the guilt themselves.

▶ARCHBISHOP FULTON J. SHEEN

It is not possible to found a lasting power upon injustice, perjury and treachery. ▶DEMOSTHENES

JELLY BEANS *See also*: LITTLE THINGS THAT MEAN A LOT

The fact is, that of all God's gifts to the sight of man, color is the holiest, the most divine, the most solemn. . . and the purest and most thoughtful minds are those which love color the most.   ▶T. S. KING

JOB ELIMINATIONS *See also*: SERVICE INDUSTRIES

Death is the dropping of the flower that the fruit may swell.
    ▶HENRY WARD BEECHER

There is no death! What seems so is transition.   ▶LONGFELLOW

JOB INTERVIEWS AND APPLICATIONS *See also*: UNEMPLOYMENT INSURANCE

It is always the best policy to tell the truth—unless, of course, you are an exceptionally good liar.   ▶JEROME K. JEROME

If you can't convince them, confuse them.   ▶PRESIDENT HARRY S. TRUMAN

Self-laudation abounds among the unpolished; but nothing can stamp a man more sharply as ill-bred.   ▶CHARLES BUXTON

Fortune befriends the bold.   ▶JOHN DRYDEN

JOB RETRAINING

There is a period of life when we go back as we advance. ▶ROUSSEAU

It is not the nature of man to keep going forward; it has its ebbs and flows. ▶PASCAL

JOY *See also*: POVERTY

Those who cannot feel pain are not capable either of feeling joy.
▶RADEN A. KARTINI

JUNK BONDS *See also*: MARKETPLACE, THE

The mind of man is ignorant of fate and destiny, and of keeping within due bounds when elated by hope of prosperity. ▶VIRGIL

JUNK MAIL

Opportunities do not come with their values stamped upon them. To face every opportunity of life thoughtfully and ask its meaning bravely and earnestly is the only way to meet the supreme opportunities when they come. ▶MALTBIE BABCOCK

JUSTICE

Justice is the soul of the universe. ▶OMAR KHAYYÁM

Who shall put his finger on the work of justice and say, "It is there"? Justice is not without us as a fact; it is within us as a great yearning.
▶GEORGE ELIOT

Justice is the constant desire and effort to render to every man his due. ▶JUSTINIAN

Justice may be blind, but she hears the gold coin that is dropped into her scales. ▶HENRIETTA FAIRCHILD

KARMA

The acts of this life are the destiny of the next. ▶INDIAN PROVERB

KINDNESS

I expect to pass through this world but once. If, therefore, there can be any kindness I can show, or any good thing I can do to any fellow being, let me do it now and not defer or neglect it, as I shall not pass this way again. ▶WILLIAM PENN

Kindness is the golden chain by which society is bound together.
▶GOETHE

Kind hearts are more than coronets, and simple faith than Norman blood. ▶ALFRED LORD TENNYSON

KINGS *See also:* JOB RETRAINING

They rise with fear, and lie with danger down;
Huge are the cares that wait upon the crown.
▶EARL OF STERLING

KISSES

Eden revives in the first kiss of love. ►Lord Byron

When a knave kisses you, count your teeth. ►Jewish proverb

KITES *See also:* Adversity

Kites rise against and not with the wind. ►John Neal

KNOWLEDGE *See also:* THINK TANKS

The love of knowledge in a young mind is almost a warrant against the infirm excitement of passions and vices. ▶HENRY WARD BEECHER

Many of the supposed increasers of knowledge have only given a new name, and often a worse, to what was well known before.
▶AUGUST W. HARE

The end of all knowledge should be virtuous action.
▶SIR PHILIP SIDNEY

LABOR

Labor, wide as the earth, has its summit in heaven. ▶Thomas Carlyle

Genius begins great works; labor alone finishes them. ▶Joseph Joubert

Hard workers are usually honest. Industry lifts them above temptation. ▶Christian N. Bovee

LANDLORDS

What we call real estate—the solid ground to build a house on—is the broad foundation on which nearly all the guilt of this world rests.

▶Nathaniel Hawthorne.

LANGUAGE See also: INFORMATION SUPERHIGHWAYS

One great use of words is to hide our thoughts. ▶Voltaire

Language was given us that we might say pleasant things to each other. ▶Christian N. Bovee

LATE BLOOMERS

The silver swan, who living had no note,
When death approached, unlocked her silent throat.

▶Anonymous

LAWS AND LAWYERS *See also:* GOVERNMENT

Laws grind the poor, and rich men rule the law. ▶OLIVER GOLDSMITH

A jury consists of twelve persons chosen to decide who has the better lawyer. ▶HOLLOWAY H. FROST

It is better to know the judge than the law. ▶JEWISH, NORSE, FRENCH, CHINESE, SPANISH, INDIAN, ITALIAN, AND RUSSIAN PROVERBS

These written laws are like spiders' webs; the small and feeble may be caught and entangled in them, but the rich and mighty force through and despise them. ▶ANARCHARSIS

LAYOFFS *See also:* POLITENESS

Certainly work is not always required of a man. There is such a thing as a sacred idleness, the cultivation of which is now fearfully neglected. ▶GEORGE MACDONALD

LAZINESS

Talk to him of Jacob's ladder and he would ask the number of steps. ▶DOUGLAS JERROLD

LEADERS

How cheerfully he seems to grin,
How neatly spreads his claws,
And welcomes little fishes in
With gently smiling jaws.
▶LEWIS CARROLL

LEAN AND MEAN

You cannot win without sacrifice.   ▶CHARLES BUXTON

Teach self-denial, and make its practice pleasurable, and you create for the world a destiny more sublime than ever issued from the brain of the wildest dreamer.   ▶SIR WALTER SCOTT

LEARNING PROCESS, THE

The world, which took but six days to make, is like to take six thousand years to make out.   ▶SIR THOMAS BROWNE

LESS IS MORE *See also:* MORE IS LESS

One girl can be pretty, but a dozen are only a chorus.

▶F. SCOTT FITZGERALD

There are better feelings than being rich, and I think a poor person can be just as happy as a rich person, depending on that person's health and family—the basics, once again. ▶DONALD TRUMP

LETTERS OF RECOMMENDATION

A pleasing figure is a perpetual letter of recommendation.

▶LORD FRANCIS BACON

LEVERAGED BUYOUTS

The wickedness of the few makes the calamity of the many.

▶PUBLIUS SYRUS

LIBERTY

Few people enjoy real liberty; we are all slaves to ideas or habits.

▶ALFRED DE MUSSET

Liberty is the right to meddle with the affairs of others. ▶ABBÉ GALEANI

LIFE AND LIFESTYLES

Life is as serious a thing as death. ▶PHILIP BAILEY

There is no wealth but life. ▶JOHN RUSKIN

While we are reasoning concerning life, life is gone. ▶DAVID HUME

Why should we have only two or three ways of life, and not thousands? ▶EMERSON

We struggle to compose an intinerary, but life insists on remaining a mystery tour. ▶EDNA FRANKLIN

That life is worth living is the most necessary of assumptions, and were it not assumed, the most impossible of conclusions. ▶GEORGE SANTAYANA

Life is like playing a violin in public and learning the instrument as one goes on. ▶SAMUEL BUTLER

LIGHT

Walk boldly and wise in that light thou hast. There is a hand above will help thee on. ▶GAMALIEL BAILEY

LIMBAUGH, RUSH

The secret of the demagogue is to make himself as stupid as his audience, so that they believe they are as clever as he. ►KARL KRAUS

To succeed in chaining the crowd you must seem to wear the same fetters. ►VOLTAIRE

LITTLE THINGS THAT MEAN A LOT, THE

Most of the critical things in life, which become the starting points of human destiny, are little things. ►ROBERT P. SMITH

Life is made up not of great sacrifices or duties but of little things, in which smiles, and kindnesses, and small obligations, given habitually, are what win and preserve the heart and secure comfort.

►SIR HUMPHREY DAVY

LOAN COMPANIES

Debt is to man what the serpent is to the bird; its eye fascinates, its breath poisons, its coil crushes sinew and bone, its jaw is the pitiless grave. ►E. G. BULWER-LYTTON

LOBBYISTS *See also:* POLITICAL ACTION COMMITTEES

Every man, however wise, needs some sagacious friend in the affairs of life. ▶PLAUTUS

LONELINESS

They are never alone that are accompanied by noble thoughts.
▶SIR PHILIP SIDNEY

LONGEVITY

Every time a man smiles, and much more when he laughs, it adds something to his fragment of life. ▶LAURENCE STERNE

LOST AND FOUND

In a better world we will find our young years and our old friends.
▶JEAN ANTOINE PETIT-SENN

LOTTERIES

The lottery of honest labor, drawn by Time, is the only one whose prizes are worth taking up and carrying home. ▶THEODORE PARKER

LOVE AND SEX

Oh! There's nothing in life like making love, except making hay in fine weather. ►ANONYMOUS

Let me dream that love goes with us to the shore unknown.
►FELICIA HEMANS

The man who leaves a woman best pleased with herself is the one whom she will soonest wish to see again. ►LA ROCHEFOUCAULD

Sex is the ersatz or substitute religion of the twentieth century.
►MALCOLM MUGGERIDGE

When we have not what we love, we must love what we have.
►ROGER DE BUSSY-RABUTIN

To a man who is incorrupt and properly constituted, woman always remains something of a mystery and a romance. He never interprets her quite literally. She, on her part, is always striving to remain a poem, and is never weary of bringing out new editions of herself in novel bindings. ►JAMES PARTON

LOVE LETTERS

A profusion of fancies and quotations is out of place in a love letter. True feeling is always direct, and never deviates into byways to cull flowers of rhetoric. ▶CHRISTIAN N. BOVEE

LUXURY

Every degree of luxury hath some connection with evil.
▶JOHN WOOLMAN

MAINSTREAM, THE

Slight not what's near through aiming at what's far. ▶Euripides

MAJOR MEDICAL

The purse of the patient often protracts his case.
▶Johann Georg Zimmerman

MALE CHAUVINISM *See also:* GLASS CEILINGS

Beard was never the true standard of brains. ▶Thomas Fuller

MANSIONS *See also:* SERVANTS AND SERVANT PROBLEMS

Our wealth is often a snare to ourselves, and always a temptation to others. ▶Caleb C. Colton

MANTRAS

Your words bring daylight with them when you speak. ▶George Eliot

MAPS

A map of the world that does not include Utopia is not worth looking at. ▶Oscar Wilde

MARKETPLACE, THE

Holiness consisteth not in a cowl or in a garment of gray. When God purifies the heart by faith, the market is sacred as well as the sanctuary.

▶MARTIN LUTHER

Each one wishes for his own advantage rather than that of others.

▶TERENCE

MARRIAGE

Are we not one? Are we not joined by heaven?
Each interwoven with the other's fate?
Are we not mixed like streams of meeting rivers
Whose blended waters are no more distinguish'd
But roll into the sea one common flood?

▶NICHOLAS ROWE

Marriage is the nursery of heaven! ▶JEREMY TAYLOR

The true way to look at marriage is as a discipline of character.

▶JAMES A. FROUDE

MCDONALD'S *See also:* WINDOWS OF OPPORTUNITY

There is always work, and tools to work with, for those who will; and blessed are the horny hands of toil.   ▶JAMES RUSSELL LOWELL

The poor eat always more relishable food than the rich; hunger makes the dishes sweet, and this occurs almost never with rich people.
▶THE MAHABHARATA

MEANING

It don't mean a thing if you ain't got that swing.   ▶DUKE ELLINGTON

How great a pity that we should not feel for what end we are born into this world till just as we are leaving it.   ▶SIR FRANCIS WALSINGHAM

MEASUREMENT

The measure of a man is the way he bears up under misfortune.
▶PLUTARCH

MEDIA CONGLOMERATES

> I am owner of the sphere,
> Of the seven stars and the solar year,
> Of Caesar's hand, and Plato's brain,
> Of Lord Christ's heart, and Shakespeare's strain.
> ▶EMERSON

MEDICAID AND MEDICARE

Take care of your health; you have no right to neglect it and thus become a burden to yourself and perhaps to others. ▶W. HALL

Help from without is often enfeebling in its effects, but help from within invariably invigorates. ▶SAMUEL SMILES

MEDITATION *See also:* UNEMPLOYMENT and UNEMPLOYMENT OFFICES

Where there is peace and meditation, there is neither anxiety nor doubt. ▶ST. FRANCIS OF ASSISI

MEETINGS

Meetings are indispensable when you don't want to do anything about a problem. ▶JOHN KENNETH GALBRAITH

MEMORY

Do you wish to be remembered? Leave a lot of debts.

▶JOHN W. RAPER

Voters quickly forget what a man says. ▶PRESIDENT RICHARD NIXON

MENTAL HEALTH

Apt words have power to assuage the tumors of a troubled mind.

▶MILTON

Generous people are rarely mentally ill. ▶KARL MENNINGER

No excellent soul is exempt from a mixture of madness. ▶ARISTOTLE

A little Madness in the Spring

Is wholesome even for the King.

▶EMILY DICKINSON

MIRACLES

We must not sit down and look for miracles. Up, and be doing, and the Lord will be with thee. ▶JOHN ELIOT

The miracles of earth are the laws of heaven. ▶LAO-TSE

MISS PIGGY

The heart of a woman is never so full of affection that there does not remain a little corner for flattery and love.   ▶Pierre Marivaux

MISTAKES

The greatest mistake you can make in life is to be continually fearing you will make one.   ▶Elbert Hubbard

MODERATION *See also:* TWINKIES

But I didn't inhale.   ▶Governor Bill Clinton

A man who has a million dollars is as well off as if he were rich.

▶John Jacob Astor

MONEY

It's good to have money and the things that money can buy, but it's good, too, to check up once in a while and make sure that you haven't lost the things that money can't buy.   ▶G. H. Lorimer

If you have money, you're wise and handsome, and you can sing.

▶Sholom Aleichem

MOONLIGHT

The loveliest faces are to be seen by moonlight, when one sees half with the eye and half with the fancy. ►CHRISTIAN N. BOVEE

MORALS AND MANNERS Do not see: CORPORATE TAKEOVERS

Wherever there is a human heart, there is an opportunity for a kindness. ►SENECA

Wise sayings often fall on barren ground; but a kind word is never thrown away. ►ARTHUR HELPS

Whatever is graceful is virtuous, and whatever is virtuous is graceful. ►CICERO

MORE IS LESS See also: LESS IS MORE

The passion to acquire riches in order to buy vain trifles corrupts the purest souls. ►ARCHBISHOP FRANCIS FENELON

The rich are like beasts of burden, carrying treasure all day, and at the night of death unladen; they carry to their grave only their bruises and marks of their toil. ►ST. AUGUSTINE

MOTHERS *See also:* CHICKEN SOUP and NANNYGATE

God could not be everywhere, and so He made mothers.

▶JEWISH SAYING

If you would reform the world from its errors and vices, begin by enlisting the mothers. ▶CHARLES SIMMONS

MOTHERS, SINGLE

Virginity is the poetry, not the reality, of life. ▶ALPHONE DE LAMARTINE

The virtue which has never been attacked by temptation is deserving of no monument. ▶MADEMOISELLE DE SCUDERI

MOTIVATION

Man acts from motives relative to his interests, and not on metaphysical speculations. ▶EDMUND BURKE.

MOUNTAIN CLIMBING *See also:* JOB RETRAINING

Our great glory consists not in never falling, but in rising every time we fall. ▶OLIVER GOLDSMITH

MUSIC *See also:* XYLOPHONES

Now the trumpet summons us again.   ▶PRESIDENT JOHN F. KENNEDY

There is music in all things, if men had ears.   ▶LORD BYRON

MUTUAL AID

God has so ordered that men, being in need of each other, should learn to love each other and bear each other's burdens.   ▶GEORGE A. SALA

MUTUAL FUNDS

Riches amassed in haste will diminish, but those gathered little by little will multiply.   ▶GOETHE

MYSTERY *See also:* GLOBAL ECONOMY

Mystery hovers over all things here below.   ▶ALPHONSE DE LAMARTINE

Some mysteries are not worth solving, but I've never known in advance which ones they are.   ▶EDNA ADAIR

The more intelligent a man is, the more mysterious life seems to him.   ▶SCHOPENHAUER

NAMES *See also:* PUBLIC RELATIONS

No greater heritage can a father bequeath to his children than a good name; nor is there in a family any richer heirlooms than the memory of a noble ancestor. ▶JAMES HAMILTON

NANNYGATE

Nobody has a more solemn duty to obey laws than those who make them. ▶SOPHOCLES

To create a public scandal is what's wicked; to sin in private is not a sin. ▶MOLIERE

NATURE AND NATURAL LIVING *See also:* HOMELESSNESS

The laws of nature are the thoughts of God. ▶ZSCHOKKE

All nature is a vast symbolism; every material fact has sheaved within it a spiritual truth. ▶EDWIN HUBBELL CHAPIN

I follow nature as the surest guide, and resign myself with obedience to her sacred laws. ▶CICERO

NECESSITIES

Our necessities are few, but our wants are endless. ▶H. W. Shaw

NEIGHBORS

How much trouble he avoids who does not look to see what his neighbor says or does or thinks. ▶Marcus Aurelius

NEPOTISM *See also:* OLD BOY NETWORKS

It is, indeed, a blessing when the virtues of noble races are hereditary. ▶Nabb

NERDS

Within the oyster's shell uncouth
The purest pearl may hide.
Trust me, you'll find a world of truth
Within that rough outside.

▶Frances S. Osgood

NETWORKING

Friendship is made fast by interwoven benefits. ▶Sir Philip Sidney

NOBILITY *See also:* BOTTOM LINES

If a man be endowed with a generous mind, this is the best kind of nobility.   ▶PLATO

NONSENSE *See also:* TALK SHOWS

A little nonsense now and then
Is relished by the wisest men.

▶ANONYMOUS

One of the unexpected results of freedom of speech in most countries is that it protects both sense and nonsense, and soon makes them indistinguishable to uneducated citizens, which is the majority of them.   ▶ANATOLE FRANCE

NORTH AMERICAN FREE TRADE AGREEMENT

The fear of one evil often leads us into a worse.   ▶NICHOLAS BOILEAU

Not trade but traits lead to riches or poverty.   ▶THE MISHNA

South of the border, down Mexico way,
That's where my job went, and it went to stay.

▶ANONYMOUS

OBSOLESCENCE

If we keep well and cheerful we are always young, and at last die in youth, even when years would count us old. ▶Tryon Edwards

OBSTACLES *See also:* KITES

The block of granite, which was an obstacle in the pathway of the weak, becomes a stepping-stone in the pathway of the strong.
▶Thomas Carlyle

OCEAN CRUISES

Only that traveling is good which reveals to me the value of home, and enables me to enjoy it better. ▶Thoreau

Drowning at sea may save you the cost of a funeral, but the fish are not going to thank you for polluting their water. ▶Toby Rust

OFFICE PARTIES

Where wildness is visible in the dance, there Satan, death and mischief are also on the floor. ▶Christian Scriver

The sooner every party breaks up, the better. ▶Jane Austen

OFFICE POLITICS AND OFFICE RELATIONS

Scrupulous people are not suited to great affairs. ▶ANNE R. J. TURGOT

The memory of past favors is like a rainbow, bright, vivid and beautiful. But it soon fades away. The memory of injuries is engraved on the heart, and remains forever. ▶THOMAS C. HALIBURTON

A man should live with his superiors as he does with his fire; not too near, lest he burn; not too far off, lest he freeze. ▶DIOGENES

OLD AGE *See also:* CORPORATE TAKEBACKS

A graceful and honorable old age is the childhood of immortality.
▶PINDAR

The soul never grows old.   ▶LONGFELLOW

The greatest comfort of my old age, and that which gives me the highest satisfaction, is the pleasing remembrance of the many benefits and friendly offices I have done to others.   ▶CATO

> What though youth gave love and roses,
> Age still leaves us friends and wine.
> ▶THOMAS MOORE

In a dream you are never eighty.   ▶ANNE SEXTON

OLD BOY NETWORKS

Old friends are best.   ▶JOHN SELDEN

Kindred interests in the preservation of good order are more important than kindred tastes in women, or even old port.
▶LORD FIELDSTONE

OP-ED PAGES *See also:* SPIN DOCTORS and THINK TANKS

O truth divine! Enlightened by thy ray, I grope and guess no more, but see my way. ►JOHN ARBUTHNOT

Men once had convictions. They now have opinions. ►HEINE

OPPORTUNITY *See also:* WINDOWS OF OPPORTUNITY and SAVINGS AND LOAN SCANDALS

To improve the golden moment of opportunity, and catch the good that is within our reach, is the great art of life. ►SAMUEL JOHNSON

A wise man will make more opportunity than he finds.

►FRANCIS LORD BACON

Everyone has a fair turn to be as great as he pleases. ►JEREMY COLLIER

Do not wait for extraordinary circumstances to do good actions; try to use ordinary situations. ►JEAN PAUL RICHTER

Next to knowing when to seize an opportunity, the most important thing in life is to know when to forego an advantage.

►BENJAMIN DISRAELI

OPTIMISM

I am an optimist. It does not seem too much use being anything else. ▶WINSTON CHURCHILL

OPULENCE *See also:* EXECUTIVE PERKS and GOLDEN PARACHUTES

Opulence is always the result of theft. If not committed by the actual possessor, then by his predecessor. ▶ST. JEROME

> Can wealth give happiness? Look round and see
> What gay distress! What splendid misery!
> Whatever fortune lavishly can pour,
> The mind annihilates and calls for more.
>
> ▶EDWARD YOUNG

OVERQUALIFIED *See also:* JOB RETRAINING

There is no mean work save that which is sordidly selfish. . . . [I]n every sphere of life the post of honor is the post of duty.

▶EDWIN H. CHAPIN

PARADISE

Paradise is open to all kind hearts. ▶Pierre Jean Béranger

A good conscience is paradise. ▶Arminius

Remembrance is the only paradise from which we cannot be driven away. ▶Jean Paul Richter

PAST, THE *See also:* OBSOLESCENCE

The world is weary of the past,
O' might it die or rest at last!

▶Shelley

PATIENCE AND PERSEVERANCE

Everything comes if a man will only wait. ▶Benjamin Disraeli

PATRIOTISM

A man's country is where the things he loves are most respected.
▶Albert Jay Nock

Patriotism is your conviction that this country is superior to all others because we were born in it. ▶George Bernard Shaw

PAY CUTS *See also:* CORPORATE TAKEBACKS. *Do not see:* EXECUTIVE PERKS and GOLDEN PARACHUTES

Men live best upon small means. Nature has provided for all, if they only know how to use her gift.　►CLAUDIANUS

PENSIONS, PRESIDENTIAL AND CONGRESSIONAL

See also: ENTITLEMENTS

Blessings ever wait on virtuous deeds, and though a little late, a sure reward succeeds.　►WILLIAM CONGREVE

PERFECTION

To live is to change, and to be perfect is to have changed often.
　　　►CARDINAL JOHN HENRY NEWMAN

The gem cannot be polished without friction, nor man perfected without trials.　►CHINESE PROVERB

PERSPECTIVE *See also:* CORPORATIONS, ANNUAL REPORTS OF

Every man takes the limit of his own field of vision for the limits of the world.　►SCHOPENHAUER

PHILANTHROPY

The rich will do everything for the poor except get off their backs.
> ▶KARL MARX

PHILOSOPHY

The discovery of what is true and the practice of that which is good are the two most important objects of philosophy. ▶VOLTAIRE

PHOTO OPPORTUNITIES

What smiles! They were the effluence of fine intellect, of true courage! ▶CHARLOTTE BRONTË

PHYSICAL FITNESS

Oh, the wild joys of living! the leaping from rock up to rock,
The strong rending of boughs from the fir tree, the
    cool silver shock
Of the plunge into the pool's living water.
> ▶ROBERT BROWNING

PINS *See also:* WINDOWS OF OPPORTUNITY

See a pin and pick it up,
All the day you'll have good luck.
>►ANONYMOUS

PLEASURES *See also:* FREEBIES

That man is the richest whose pleasures are the cheapest.
>►THOREAU

The chief secret of comfort lies in not suffering trifles to vex us, and in prudently cultivating an undergrowth of small pleasures, since very few great ones are let on long leases. ►AUGHEY

POETRY

Poetry is not to be found unless we carry it within us. ►JOSEPH JOUBERT

POLITENESS *See also:* LAYOFFS

Politeness is a wreath of flowers that adorns the world.
>►MME. DE BASSANVILLE

There is no accomplishment so easy to acquire as politeness, and none more profitable. ►H. W. SHAW

POLITICAL ACTION COMMITTEES *See also:* GOVERNMENT

The more we give to others, the more we are increased.
▶LAO-TSE

Whoever makes great presents, expects great presents in return.
▶MARTIAL

POLITICAL CANDIDATES

Whenever a man has cast a longing eye on offices, a rottenness begins in his conduct.   ▶PRESIDENT THOMAS JEFFERSON

In public life, what divides ambitious men is not so much their dedication to ideas as their competition for office and its spoils.
▶RED KIMMEL

POLITICAL CORRECTNESS

To let politics become a cesspool, and then avoid it because it is a cesspool, is a double crime.   ▶HOWARD CROSBY

You have not converted a man because you have silenced him.
▶JOHN MORLEY

POLITICS, POWER AND GOVERNMENT

Politics is supposed to be the second oldest profession. I have come to realize that it bears a very close resemblance to the first.

▶President Ronald Reagan

No government man can be just a little crooked.

▶President Herbert Hoover

In order to become the master, the politician poses as the servant.

▶Charles de Gaulle

Idealism is the noble toga that political gentlemen drape over their will to power. ▶Aldous Huxley

In politics, nothing is contemptible. ▶Benjamin Disraeli

Power is ever stealing from the many to give to the few.

▶Wendell Phillips

If you do not know how to lie, cheat, and steal, turn your attention to politics and learn. ▶H. W. Shaw

During the whole of human history, it is not the workers but the robbers who have been in control of the world. ►SCOTT NEARING

There is an infinity of political errors which, being once adopted, become principles. ►ABBÉ RAYNAL

Politics resembles religion; attempting to divest either of ceremony is the most certain mode of bringing either into contempt.
►OLIVER GOLDSMITH

Trust not him that seems a saint. ►THOMAS FULLER

POLLS *See also*: REPUTATION

It often happens that those of whom we speak least on earth are best known in heaven. ►NICOLAS CAUSSIN

If it has to choose who is to be crucified, the crowd will always save Barabas. ►JEAN COCTEAU

What the heart wishes, the mind believes. ►C. E. LUTHARDT

The only things that polls ever prove is that people keep changing their minds. ►ELLIS WEEDE

POPULARITY

A true man never frets about his place in the world, but just slides into it by the gravitation of his nature, and swings there as easily as a star. ▶EDWIN HUBBELL CHAPIN

POSSESSIONS *See also:* FREEBIES

All of our possessions are as nothing compared to health, strength, and a clear conscience. ▶HOSEA BALLOU

An honest heart possesses a kingdom. ▶SENECA

There are many things that are thorns to our hopes until we have attained them, and envenomed arrows to our hearts when we have.

▶HONORÉ DE MIRABEAU

The more a man lays stress on false possessions, and the less sensitivity he has for what is essential, the less satisfying is his life.

▶CARL JUNG

POSTINDUSTRIAL SOCIETY *See also:* MCDONALD'S

So long as the increased wealth which modern progress brings goes but to build up great fortunes, to increase luxury and make sharper the contrast between the House of Have and the House of Want, progress is not real and cannot be permanent. ►HENRY GEORGE

POVERTY *See also:* JOY

Poverty, when it is voluntary, is never despicable, but takes an heroical aspect. ►HAZLITT

Where there is poverty and joy, there is neither greed nor avarice.
►ST. FRANCIS OF ASSISI

Poverty is the test of civility and the touchstone of friendship.
►HAZLITT

To crave more than you need—that is poverty. ►I. V. PANIN

POWER

To have what we want is riches, but to be able to do without it is power. ►GEORGE MACDONALD

PRAYER

Prayer moves the hand which moves the world. ▶J. A. WALLACE

No man ever prayed heartily without learning something. ▶EMERSON

In prayer it is better to have a heart without words than words without a heart. ▶JOHN BUNYAN

Pray not too often for great favors, for we stand most in need of small ones. ▶J. L. BASFORD

In all times and in all countries the great majority of mankind find it easier to beg their way to heaven with prayers than to deserve to go there by their actions. ▶SCHOPENHAUER

PRESIDENTS *See also:* SPIN DOCTORS

True statesmanship is the art of changing a nation from what it is into what it ought to be. ▶WILLIAM R. ALGER

I'd rather be right than be President, but once elected, I probably wouldn't be so fastidious. ▶HENRY VENTER

PRESIDENTIAL DEBATES

A little inaccuracy sometimes saves tons of explanation. ▶SAKI

To murder character is as truly a crime as to murder the body; the tongue of the slanderer is brother to the dagger of the assassin.

▶TRYON EDWARDS

PRIDE

From the gilded saloon to the bier and the shroud,
Oh, why should the spirit of mortal be proud?

▶WILLIAM KNOX

Poverty is no disgrace, but neither can you be proud of it. ▶Lazerov

PRISONS *See also:* MANSIONS

We pass our life in forging fetters for ourselves, and in complaining of having to wear them. ▶GASTON VAPOREAU

PRIVATE CLUBS *See also:* GLASS CEILINGS

All amusements to which virtuous women are not admitted are, rely upon it, deleterious in their nature. ▶THACKERAY

PRIVATE SECTOR, THE

People of the same trade seldom meet together, even for merriment and diversion, but their conversation ends in a conspiracy against the public, or in some contrivance to raise prices. ▶ADAM SMITH

PRIVILEGE *See also:* REVOLUTIONS

People of privilege will always risk their complete destruction rather than surrender any material part of their advantage.

▶JOHN KENNETH GALBRAITH

PROFESSIONS, THE

All professions are conspiracies against the laity.

▶GEORGE BERNARD SHAW

PROFIT MOTIVE, THE *See also:* PRIVATE SECTOR, THE

For what is a man profited if he shall gain the whole world and lose his own soul? ▶MATTHEW 16:26

PROGRESS *See also:* CORPORATE MERGERS and SYNERGY

Is it progress when a cannibal uses knife and fork? ▶FANNY H. LEA

Progress is the mother of problems. ▶G. K. CHESTERTON

What we call "progress" is the exchange of one nuisance for another.
▶HAVELOCK ELLIS

PROPERTY

Few rich men own their own property. The property owns them.
▶ROBERT G. INGERSOLL

Wherever there is great property there is great inequality. For one rich man there must be at least five hundred poor, and the affluence of the few supposes the indigence of the many. ▶ADAM SMITH

What the heart has once owned and had, it shall never lose.
▶HENRY WARD BEECHER

PROSPERITY

Prosperity often presages adversity. ▶HOSEA BALLOU

Prosperity engenders sloth. ▶LIVY

PROVIDENCE

The providence that watches over the affairs of men works out of their mistakes, at times, a healthier issue than could have been accomplished by their own wisest forethought. ▶JAMES A. FROUDE

PROZAC

A man he seems of cheerful yesterdays and confident tomorrows.
▶WORDSWORTH

The habit of looking on the best side of every event is worth more than a thousand pounds a year. ▶SAMUEL JOHNSON

PSYCHOTHERAPY

Go to your bosom;
Knock there, and ask your heart what it doth know.
▶SHAKESPEARE

A wonderful discovery—psychoanalysis. It makes simple people feel they're complex. ▶S. N. BEHRMAN

PUBLIC OPINION *See also:* TALK SHOWS

There is no tyranny so despotic as public opinion among a free people. ►DONN PIATT

PUBLIC RELATIONS *See also:* SPIN DOCTORS

We do what we must and call it by the best names. ►EMERSON

If an idiot were to tell you the same story every day for a year, you would end by believing him. ►EDMUND BURKE

A pleasant illusion is better than a harsh reality. ►CHRISTIAN N. BOVEE

There is no calamity which right words will not begin to redress. ►EMERSON

PUNCTUALITY

People count up the faults of those who keep them waiting. ►FRENCH PROVERB

PUNDITS

It is by no means necessary to understand things to speak confidently about them. ►BEAUMARCHAIS

QUACKS *See also:* HEALTH INSURANCE

If he says that his elixir will not only cure your lumbago but make you look like Rudolph Valentino, chances are that he's just a quack.

▶RALPH OATES

QUADRILLES *See also:* JOB INTERVIEWS

Learn to dance, not so much for the sake of dancing, as for coming into a room and presenting yourself genteelly and gracefully. Women, whom you ought to endeavor to please, cannot forgive a vulgar and awkward air and gesture. ▶LORD CHESTERFIELD

QUALITY

Quality, not quantity, is my measure. ▶DOUGLAS JERROLD

Nothing endures but personal qualities. ▶WHITMAN

QUALMS

I don't like these cold, precise, perfect people who, in order not to speak wrong, never speak at all, and in order not to do wrong, never do anything. ▶HENRY WARD BEECHER

QUANDRIES

When we cannot act as we wish, we must act as we can. ►Terrence

QUARANTINE

They are never alone who are accompanied with noble thoughts.
►Sir Philip Sidney

QUEUES

All good abides with him who waiteth wisely. ►Thoreau

QUIETNESS

A gentleman makes no noise, a lady is serene. ►Emerson

QUILLS *See also:* WORDS AND WORD PROCESSING

Quills are things that are sometimes taken from the pinions of one goose to spread the opinions of another. ►Paul Chatfield

QUILTING BEES

Good company and good discourse are the very sinews of virtue.
►Izaak Walton

QUOTATIONS

The wisdom of the wise and the experience of the ages may be preserved by quotation. ▸BENJAMIN DISRAELI

Precepts or maxims are of great weight, and a few useful ones at hand do more toward a happy life than whole volumes that we know not where to find. ▸SENECA

RAINBOWS *See also*: SUPPORT SYSTEMS

Be thou the rainbow to the storms of life, the evening beam that smiles the clouds away and tints tomorrow with prophetic ray.

▶LORD BYRON

REACHING OUT

The drying up a single tear has more
Of honest fame than shedding seas of gore.

▶LORD BYRON

Great minds, like heaven, are pleased in doing good, though the ungrateful subjects of their favors are barren in return. ▶NICHOLAS ROWE

READING *See also*: WANT ADS and SELF-HELP BOOKS

No entertainment is so cheap as reading, nor any pleasure so lasting. ▶LADY MARY WORTLEY MONTAGUE

REASON *See also*: WISDOM

It is useless to attempt to reason a man out of a thing he was never reasoned into. ▶JONATHAN SWIFT

RECYCLING *See also*: RESURRECTION

Those who cannot remember the past are condemned to repeat it.
▶GEORGE SANTAYANA

RED INK *See also*: BANKRUPTCY

Losses are comparative. It is only imagination that makes them of any significance. ▶PASCAL

REFINEMENT

It is in refinement and elegance that the civilized man differs from the savage. ▶SAMUEL JOHNSON

REGRET

We often regret we did not do otherwise when that very otherwise would, in all probability, have done for us. ▶CHARLES CALEB COLTON

REJECTION *See also*: DOGS and PSYCHOTHERAPY

One of the mistakes in the conduct of human life is to suppose that other men's opinions are to make us happy. ▶RICHARD E. BURTON

RELATIVITY

Poverty is relative, and, therefore, not ignoble.

▶E. G. Bulwer-Lytton

RELAXATION

There is no joy but calm. ▶Tennyson

RELIGION

Money degrades all the gods of man and converts them into commodities. ▶Karl Marx

A religious life is a struggle and not a hymn. ▶Madame de Staël

If men are so wicked with religion, what would they be without it?

▶Ben Franklin

Christianity might be a good thing if anyone ever tried it.

▶George Bernard Shaw

REPOSSESSION *See also:* SACRIFICE

Heaven sends us misfortunes as a moral tonic.

▶Lady Marguerite Blessington

REPUTATION

Reputation is what men and women think of us; character is what God and angels know of us. ▶THOMAS PAINE

A reputation for good judgment, fair dealing, truth and rectitude is itself a fortune. ▶HENRY WARD BEECHER

REST AND RECREATION

God gives quietness at last. ▶WHITTIER

Sprinkled along the waste of years
Full many a soft green isle appears;
Pause where we may upon the desert road,
Some shelter is in sight, some sacred safe abode.

▶JOHN KEBLE

RESUMES *See also:* PUBLIC RELATIONS. *Do not see:* SHYNESS

If you have it, flaunt it. If you don't have it, flaunt it anyway.

▶QUOTED BY JULIETTE PROUSE

To myself alone do I owe my fame. ▶CORNEILLE

Song forbids victorious deeds to die. ▶SCHILLER

RESURRECTION

In our anxiety over our death and resurrection, we tend to forget that we are resurrected every morning. ▶MORRIS STERN

RETIREMENT

Work is a symbol of conflict and discord; rest is an expression of dignity, peace and freedom. ▶ERIC FROMM

> Now is done thy long day's toil,
> Fold thy palms across thy breast,
> Fold thy arms, turn to thy rest.
>
> ▶TENNYSON

REVOLUTIONS

The best security against revolution lies in constant correction of abuses and the introduction of needed improvements. ▶BISHOP WHATELY

If we permit extremes of wealth for a few and enduring poverty for many, we shall create a social explosiveness and a demand for revolutionary change. ▶PRESIDENT DWIGHT D. EISENHOWER

ROLE MODELS

People seldom improve when they have no other model but themselves to copy after. ▶OLIVER GOLDSMITH

FEMALE ROLE MODELS

What is beauty? Not the show
Of shapely limbs and features. No.
They are but flowers
That have their dated hours
To breathe their momentary sweets, then go.
'Tis the stainless soul within
That outshines the fairest skin.

▶SIR ALFRED HUNT

MALE ROLE MODELS

Rugged strength and radiant beauty—
These were one in Nature's plan;
Humble toil and heavenward duty—
These will form the perfect man.

▶SARAH J. HALE

ROMANCE NOVELS

I like them because the heroine always gets the hero. Best of all, the story ends at just the right time, either before marriage or as the couple leave on their honeymoon. ▶MINDY RYAN

ROYALTY *See also:* UNEMPLOYMENT OFFICES

Uneasy lies the head that wears a crown. ▶SHAKESPEARE

Every noble crown is, and on earth will forever be, a crown of thorns.
▶THOMAS CARLYLE

SACRIFICE

Who lives for humanity must be content to lose himself.
►O. B. Frothingham

We can all offer up a great deal in the large, but to make sacrifices in the little things is what we are seldom equal to. ►Goethe

SAFETY NETS *See also:* SUPPORT SYSTEMS and PROZAC

I wrap myself up in my virtue. ►Horace

It is one of the worst of errors to suppose that there is any path of safety except that of duty. ►William Nevins

SAINTS

Every once in a while some feller without a single bad habit gets caught. ►Frank McKinney Hubbard

The way of the world is to praise dead saints, and persecute living ones. ►Nathaniel Howe

SALESMEN *See also:* POLITICAL CANDIDATES

Scoundrels are always sociable. ►Schopenhauer

SAVINGS AND LOAN SCANDALS

Every temptation is great or small according as the man is.
►Jeremy Taylor

Life is the art of being well-deceived. ►William Hazlitt

The art of winning in business is to pray hard, work hard, and hire the best lobbyists in Washington. ►Jason Gray

When private virtue is hazarded on the perilous cast of expediency, the pillars of the republic, however apparent their stability, are infected with decay at the very centre. ►Edwin Hubbell Chapin

SEASONS, THE

When spring unlocks the flowers to paint the laughing soil;
When summer's balmy showers refresh the mower's toil;
When winter binds in frosty chains the fallow and the flood,
In God the earth rejoiceth still, and owns his Maker good.
►Bishop Reginald Heber

SECOND CAREERS

If you're the sort of doctor who kills more patients than he cures, maybe your real talent is for undertaking. ▶ELLIS CRANE

SECURITY

There is nothing perfectly secure but poverty. ▶LONGFELLOW

Uncertainty and expectation are joys of life. Security is an insipid thing, and the overtaking and possession of a wish discovers the folly of the chase. ▶WILLIAM CONGREVE

SELF-DEFENSE

We cannot control the evil tongues of others, but a good life enables us to despise them. ▶CATO

SELF-DENIAL

The more a man denies himself, the more he shall receive from heaven. ▶HORACE

SELF-EMPLOYMENT

Hail, independence, hail! Heaven's next best gift to that of life and an immortal soul! ▶JAMES THOMSON

SELF-HELP AND SELF-HELP BOOKS

Help thyself, and God will help thee. ▶GEORGE HERBERT

It is necessary to keep trying to improve yourself. This occupation ought to last all your life. ▶QUEEN CHRISTIANA OF SWEDEN

Books—lighthouses erected in the great sea of time.
▶HENRY B. WHIPPLE

Books are those faithful mirrors that reflect to our mind the minds of sages and heroes. ▶EDWARD GIBBON

Human improvement is from within outwards. ▶JAMES A. FROUDE

Begin to be this moment what you want to be hereafter.
▶ST. JEROME

SELF-RESPECT

To have a respect for ourselves guides our morals, and to have a deference for others governs our manners. ▶LAURENCE STERNE

SERVANTS AND SERVANT PROBLEMS *See also*: NANNYGATE

Expect not more from servants than is just;
Reward them well, if they observe their trust.
►SIR JOHN DENHAM

Be not too familiar with thy servants; at first it may beget love, but in the end 'twill breed contempt. ►THOMAS FULLER

SERVICE INDUSTRIES *See also*: SECOND CAREERS

They serve God well,
Who serve His creatures.
►CAROLINE NORTON

SESAME STREET *See also*: TWINKIES

Mental pleasures never cloy. Unlike those of the body, they are increased by repetition, approved by reflection, and strengthened by enjoyment. ►CALEB C. COLTON

All pleasures are commendable that do not culminate in regret.
►MADAME DE MAINTENON

SEX

If sensuality were happiness, beasts would be happier than men, but human felicity is lodged in the soul and not in the flesh. ►SENECA

SHADOWS *See also:* MUTUAL FUNDS

What shadows we are, and what shadows we pursue! ►EDMUND BURKE

SHELTERS, PUBLIC

Send these, the homeless, tempest tossed, to me.

I lift my lamp beside the golden door.

►EMMA LAZARUS, INSCRIPTION ON THE STATUE OF LIBERTY

Sprinkled along the waste of years

Full many a soft green isle appears;

Pause where we may upon the desert road,

Some shelter is in sight, some sacred safe abode.

►JOHN KEBLE

SHOPPING LISTS

The more a man denies himself, the more he shall receive from God.

►HORACE

SHORT-TERM PROFITS

Cease to inquire what the future has in store, and take as a gift whatever the day brings forth. ▶HORACE

SHYNESS

If men knew all that women think, they would be twenty times more audacious. ▶ALPHONSE KARR

SILENCE *See also:* TALK SHOWS

True silence is the rest of the mind, and is to the spirit what sleep is to the body—nourishment and refreshment. It is a great virtue; it covers folly, keeps secrets, avoids disputes, and prevents sin.

▶WILLIAM PENN

There are some silent people who are more interesting than the best talkers. ▶BENJAMIN DISRAELI

SIMPLE LIFE, THE

There is majesty in simplicity. ▶ALEXANDER POPE

Plain living and high thinking. ▶WORDSWORTH

SIN

Charity shall cover a multitude of sins. ►1 PETER 4:8

SLEEP

Sleep, to the homeless thou art home; the friendless find a friend in thee. ►EBENEZER ELLIOTT

Put off thy cares with thy clothes; so shall thy rest strengthen thy labor; and so shall thy labor sweeten thy rest. ►FRANCIS QUARLES

SMILES

The face that cannot smile is never fair.   ▶MARTIAL

A lot of our candidates have only a smile going for them. But usually that's enough for our voters.   ▶ANONYMOUS

In America you must live life with a smile, even before your toothbrush reaches your mouth.   ▶PRINCE WILLIAM OF SWEDEN

SMILIN' THROUGH *See also:* ADVERSITY

Not now but in the coming years,
It may be in the better land,
We'll read the meaning of our tears,
And there, some time, we'll understand.

▶MAXWELL X. CORNELIUS

SOAP OPERAS *See also:* SPIN DOCTORS

The taste for emotion may become a dangerous taste; we should be very cautious how we attempt to squeeze out of human life more ecstacy and paroxysm than it can well afford.   ▶SYDNEY SMITH

SOCIAL CONTRACTS *See also:* REPOSSESSION

The big print giveth and the fine print taketh away.
>►ARCHBISHOP J. FULTON SHEEN

The most obvious division of society is into rich and poor, and it is no less obvious that the number of the former bear a great disproportion to those of the latter. The whole business of the poor is to administer to the idleness, folly, and the luxury of the rich, and that of the rich, in return, is to find the best methods of confirming the slavery and increasing the burdens of the poor. ►EDMUND BURKE

SOCIAL SECURITY

Make all you can, save all you can, give all you can. ►JOHN WESLEY

He who wishes to secure the good of others has already secured himself. ►CONFUCIUS

SOCIETY

It is the wretchedness of being rich that you have to live with rich people. ►LOGAN P. SMITH

SOLVENCY *See also:* ANTS

Solvency is entirely a matter of temperament and not of income.
▶LOGAN P. SMITH

SOULS

The lack of wealth is easily repaired; but the poverty of the soul is irreparable.   ▶MONTAIGNE

SOUND BITES

Men are led by trifles.   ▶NAPOLEON

"I love you" was probably the first sound bite. But it's still the best.
▶SYLVIA COOPER

SOUP KITCHENS, FREE

One meal a day is enough for a lion, and it ought to be for a man.
▶DR. GEORGE FORDYCE

For the earl in ermine or the char in cloth,

There's nothing more wholesome than bread and broth.

▶MARGARET TROTTER

SPICES

Spices and suchlike embellishments do not add any nourishment to the simple and wholesome fare that Nature has provided for men and women. Columbus discovered America when he set out in quest of ginger and cinnamon in 1492, and historians are still debating the long-term benefits of his journey. ▶ABBÉ REINAL

SPIN DOCTORS

Pour the full tide of eloquence along,
Serenely pure and yet divinely strong.

▶ALEXANDER POPE

I always tried to turn every disaster into an opportunity.

▶JOHN D. ROCKEFELLER

No virtue looks small when it is properly staged. ▶JOSEPH JOUBERT

SPREADSHEETS

The study of the properties of numbers, Plato tells us, habituates the mind to the contemplation of pure truth, and raises us above the material universe. ▶THOMAS B. MACAULAY

STARS

If the stars should appear one night in a thousand years, how would men believe and adore; and preserve for many generations the remembrance of the city of God which had been shown! But every night come out these envoys of beauty, and light the universe with their admonishing smile. ►EMERSON

STATISTICS *See also:* PROFIT MOTIVE, THE

It is a statistical fact that the wicked work harder to reach hell than the righteous do to enter heaven. ►H. W. SHAW

Statistics are no substitute for judgment. ►HENRY CLAY

STATUS

The moment the slave resolves that he will no longer be a slave, his fetters fall. He frees himself and shows the way to others. Freedom and slavery are mental states. ►GANDHI

STOCKS AND STOCK MARKETS

I dwell in Possibility. ▶EMILY DICKINSON

All human things hang on a slender thread; the strongest fall with a sudden crash. ▶OVID

SUCCESS

Success often costs more than it is worth. ▶EDWARD WIGGLESWORTH

We can do anything we want to do if we stick to it long enough.

▶HELEN KELLER

SUICIDE *See also:* HOMELESSNESS

When all the blandishments of life are gone,
The coward sneaks to death, the brave live on.

▶GEORGE SEWELL

To die in order to avoid the pains of poverty, love, or anything that is disagreeable, is not the part of a brave man but of a coward.

▶ARISTOTLE

SUNSETS *See also*: CONTENTMENT

The setting sun is reflected as brightly from the windows of the almshouse as from the rich man's abode. ►THOREAU

SUPERMARKET FLIERS AND COUPONS

These papers of the day have uses more adequate to the purposes of common life than more pompous and durable volumes.

►SAMUEL JOHNSON

SUPERNATURAL, THE

Can the supernatural be more incredible than something we consider perfectly natural, such as the billions of neurons in the brain of the average scientist? ►PHYLLIS MICHEL

SUPERSTARS *See also*: ROYALTY

Shrines to burn earth's incense on, the altar fires of heaven!

►WHITTIER

Surely the stars are images of love. ►PHILIP J. BAILEY

SUPPORT SYSTEMS

> Life's morn will soon be waning,
> And its evening bells be tolled,
> But my heart shall know no sadness,
> If you'll love me when I'm old.
>
> ►Anonymous

SUPREME COURT, U.S.

All should bow to virtue, and then walk far away from it.

►J. de Finod

We are under a Constitution, but the Constitution is what the judges say it is. ►Chief Justice Charles Evans Hughes

SUSHI *See also:* ZEN

Never lick your chopsticks to get at the last grains of rice sticking to them. ►Japanese etiquette pamphlet

SWEETHEARTS

Nobody's sweetheart is ugly. ►J. J. Vadé

SYMPATHY *See also:* OLD BOY NETWORKS

True sympathy is beyond what can be seen and touched and reasoned upon. ►MRS. CAMPBELL PRAED

We only truly sympathize with misfortunes such as we have ourselves undergone. ►COMTESSE DIANE

SYNERGY

It is one of the most beautiful compensations of this life that no man can sincerely try to help another without helping himself. ►UNKNOWN

Light is the task where many share the toil. ►HOMER

Little deeds of kindness, little words of love,
Make our earth an Eden, like the heaven above.
►JULIA A. CARNEY

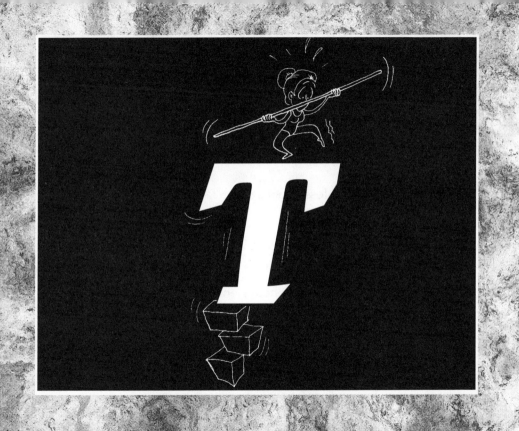

TABLOID JOURNALISM *See also:* SOAP OPERAS

A few vices are sufficient to darken many virtues. ►PLUTARCH

TALK SHOWS AND TALK-SHOW HOSTS

We often say things because we can say them well rather than because they are sound and reasonable. ►WALTER SAVAGE LANDOR

TASTE

Taste is pursued at a less expense than fashion.
►WILLIAM SHENSTONE

TAXES AND TAX REFORM

Death and taxes are inevitable. ►THOMAS C. HALIBURTON

The taxes of government are heavy enough, but not as heavy as the taxes we lay upon ourselves. ►ORVILLE DEWEY

When President and Congress want to lower the taxes of their wealthy supporters, they sock it to the middle class and call it tax reform. ►JACK SPOFFORD

TAXES, PENALTY FOR LATE PAYMENT OF ESTIMATED

Promptness is the soul of business. ▶Lord Chesterfield

Better three hours too soon than one minute too late. ▶Shakespeare

TEA *See also:* LITTLE THINGS THAT MEAN A LOT

Love and scandals are the best sweeteners of tea. ▶Henry Fielding

There are few hours in life more agreeable than the hour dedicated to the ceremony known as afternoon tea. ▶Henry James

TELEVISION

The mind ought sometimes to be diverted, that it may return the better to thinking. ▶Phaedrus

Most pleasures embrace us but to strangle. ▶Montaigne

TELEVISION EVANGELISTS AND TELEVISION PERSONALITIES

Avoid, as you would the plague, a clergyman who is also a man of business. ▶St. Jerome

These preachers of beauty, which light the world with their admonishing smile. ▶Emerson

TEMPTATION

Honest bread is very well. It's the butter that makes the temptation.
►Douglas Jerrold

TERM PAPERS *See also*: RESUMES

There are greater depths and obscurities, greater intricacies and perplexities, in an elaborate and well-written piece of nonsense than in the most abstruse and profound tract of school divinity. ►Joseph Addison

THANKSGIVING DAY

Our lives are environed with God's goodness. We sleep in the midst of untouched harps of blessing. Let us arise and sweep their strings on this Thanksgiving Day. ►Rev. David J. Burrell

THERAPISTS

It is easier to be wise for others than for ourselves.
►La Rochefoucauld

THINKING

A great many people think they are thinking when they are rearranging their prejudices. ►William James

THINK TANKS

This wisdom would send Solomon back to the schoolroom.

▶SHAKESPEARE

Bull permeates everything.   ▶LEE ATWATER

A true scholar will objectively study all sides of a problem before coming to the conclusion desired by his patron.   ▶FRIEDA TIECK

THRIFT *See also*: BOTTOM LINES; *Do not see*: EXECUTIVE PERKS

Large enterprises make the few rich, but the majority prosper only through the carefulness and detail of thrift. He is already poverty-stricken whose habits are not thrifty.   ▶T. T. MURGER

THRIFT SHOPS

If I have ever made any valuable discoveries, it has been owing more to patient attention than to any other talent.

▶SIR ISAAC NEWTON

TIME

> One day with life and heart,
>
> Is more than time enough to find a world.
>
> ►JAMES RUSSELL LOWELL

Time is a wave that never murmurs, because there is no obstacle to its flow.   ►MADAME SWETCHINE

> Redeem the misspent time that's past,
>
> And live this day as 'twere thy last.
>
> ►ANONYMOUS

What lies before you and what lies behind you are tiny matters compared to what lies within you.   ►EMERSON

TOBACCO SUBSIDIES *See also:* SAFETY NETS and SAVINGS AND LOAN SCANDALS and PENSIONS, PRESIDENTIAL AND CONGRESSIONAL

Many people consider the things government does for them to be social progress, but they regard the things government does for others as socialism.   ►U.S. SUPREME COURT CHIEF JUSTICE EARL WARREN

TOGETHERNESS

What is the grave to us? Can it divide
The destiny of two made one?
We step across, and reach the other side,
To know our blended life is but begun.
These fading faculties are sent to say
Heaven is more near today than yesterday.

▶S. C. HALL

TOLERANCE

Forbear to judge, for we are sinners all.　▶SHAKESPEARE

I never hated a man enough to give him his diamonds back.

▶ZSA ZSA GABOR

TOWN AND COUNTRY

The lowest and vilest alleys of London do not present a more dreadful record of sin than does the smiling and beautiful countryside.

▶SIR ARTHUR CONAN DOYLE

TRACK RECORDS

I have fought a good fight, I have finished my course, I have kept the faith. ▶2 TIMOTHY 4:7

TRANSPORTATION AND TRAVEL

The great thing in this world is not where we are, but in what direction we are moving. ▶OLIVER WENDELL HOLMES

To travel hopefully is better than to arrive, and the true success is to labor. ▶ROBERT LOUIS STEVENSON

TRIALS AND TRIBULATIONS

Trials teach us what we are. ►CHARLES H. SPURGEON

Life has no smooth road for any of us; and in the bracing atmosphere of a high aim, the very roughness only stimulates the climber to steadier and steadier steps. ►BISHOP W. C. DOANE

The true way to soften one's troubles is to solace those of others.

►MADAME DE MAINTENON

In this wild world the fondest and the best are the most tried, the most troubled and distressed. ►GEORGE CRABBE

TRUTH

The terrible thing about the quest for truth is that you find it.

►REMY DE GOURMONT

Every violation of truth is a stab at the health of human society.

►EMERSON

Truth, like a bird, is ever poised for flight at man's approach.

►JEAN BROWN

TWILIGHT *See also:* RETIREMENT and SOCIAL SECURITY

> Peacefully
> The quiet stars came out, one after one;
> The holy twilight fell upon the sea,
> The summer day was done.
>> ►CELIA THAXTER

TWINKIES™

Tranquil pleasures last the longest. We are not fitted to bear long the burden of great joys. ►CHRISTIAN N. BOVEE

Tell me what you eat, and I will tell you what you are.
>> ►BRILLAT SAVARIN

TYRANNY

Of all forms of tyranny, the least attractive and the most vulgar is the tyranny of wealth, the tyranny of plutocracy. ►J. P. MORGAN

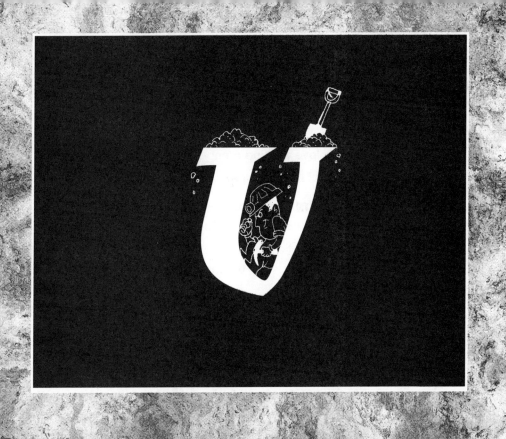

UGLINESS

Better an ugly face than an ugly mind. ▶James Ellis

UNEMPLOYMENT

When more and more people are thrown out of work, unemployment results. ▶President Calvin Coolidge

The man who falls in love will find plenty of occupation. ▶Ovid

Ah, why should life all labor be? ▶Alfred Lord Tennyson

UNEMPLOYMENT INSURANCE AND UNEMPLOYMENT OFFICES

It is not designed that the road should be made too smooth for us here on earth. ▶Jane Porter

The greater our dread of crosses, the more necessary they are for us.
▶François Fénelon

UNITED NATIONS, THE

And the kindly earth shall slumber, lapped in universal law.
▶Alfred Lord Tennyson

UNITED STATES, THE

Let our object be our country, our whole country, and nothing but our country. And, by the blessing of God, may that country itself become a vast and splendid monument, not of oppression and terror, but of wisdom, of peace, and of liberty, upon which the world may gaze with admiration forever. ▶DANIEL WEBSTER

UNKNOWN, THE

Heaven makes sport of human affairs, and the present hour gives no sure promise of the next. ▶OVID

> I think of death as some delightful journey
> That I shall take when all my tasks are done.
> ▶ELLA WHEELER WILCOX

UPTIGHT

Good temper, like a sunny day, sheds a brightness over everything; it is the sweetener of toil and the soother of disquietude.
▶WASHINGTON IRVING

UPWARD MOBILITY

No influence so quickly converts a radical into a reactionary as does his election to power. ▶Elizabeth Marbury

Nobody is so cruel as a man raised from lowly station to prosperity. ▶Ovid

URBANITY

Better were it to be unborn than ill bred. ▶Sir Walter Raleigh

Let there be many windows to your soul, that all the glory of the world may beautify it. ▶Ella Wheeler Wilcox

USEFULNESS

Those men and women are fortunate who are born at a time when a great struggle for human freedom is in progress. ▶Emmeline Pankhurst

Do not wait for extraordinary circumstances to do good actions. Try to use ordinary situations. ▶John Paul Richter

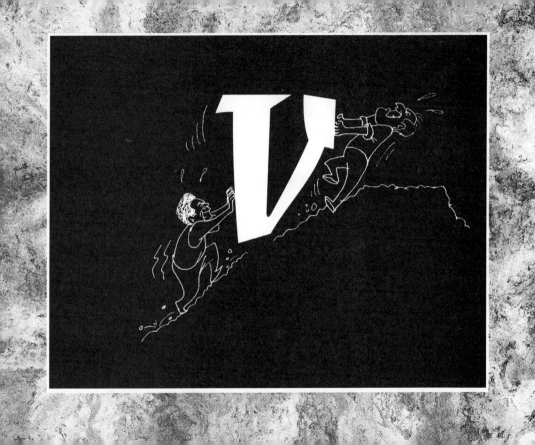

VAGRANTS

A vagrant is everywhere at home. ▶MARTIAL

VALENTINE'S DAY

And now the lads and lasses, following the example of the birds, bill and coo together. ▶H. W. SHAW

VALOR *See also*: BAG LADIES

Valor is stability, not of arms and of legs, but of courage and the soul. ▶MONTAIGNE

VARIETY

Variety alone gives joy,
The sweetest meats the soonest cloy.

▶MATTHEW PRIOR

VICE *See also*: DOWNSIZING and LAYOFFS

The vices of the rich and great are mistaken for errors; and those of the poor and lowly, for crimes. ▶LADY BLESSINGTON.

If the wicked flourish and you suffer, be not discouraged; they are being fatted for destruction, you are being dieted for health.

▶THOMAS FULLER

VICTORY *See also*: JOB INTERVIEWS

Victories that are easy are cheap. Those only are worth having which come as the result of hard fighting. ▶HENRY WARD BEECHER

VIDEO TAPES *See also*: LOVE and SEX

Recreation is not the highest kind of enjoyment, but in its time and place is quite as proper as prayer. ▶S. I. PRIME

VIRTUAL REALITY

A lie has always a certain amount of weight with those who wish to believe it. ▶ELLIOTT W. RICE

VIRTUE

Virtue is its own reward, and brings with it the truest and highest pleasure. ▶CARDINAL JOHN HENRY NEWMAN

However virtuous a woman may be, a compliment on her virtue is what gives her the least pleasure. ▶PRINCE DE LIGNE

VIRUSES *See also:* MAJOR MEDICAL

Sickness puts us in mind of our mortality, and while we drive on heedlessly in the full career of worldly pomp and jollity, she kindly pulls us by the ear and brings us to a proper sense of our duty.

▶ROBERT BURTON

VOODOO ECONOMICS

Worldly wealth is the devil's bait. ▶ROBERT BURTON

To know how to dissemble is the knowledge of rulers.

▶CARDINAL RICHELIEU

VULGARITY

Success will popularize the grossest vulgarity. ▶ALFRED BOUGEART

WALKING See also: FAST TRACK, THE

Life is a maze in which we take the wrong turning before we have learnt to walk. ▶CYRIL CONNOLLY

Walk in the light and thou shalt see thy path though it be thorny.
▶BRUCE BARTON

WANT ADS

Turn to the press—its teeming sheets survey,
Big with the wonders of each passing day.
▶CHARLES SPRAGUE

WATER See also: WINE

Drinking water neither makes a man sick, nor in debt, nor his wife a widow. ▶JOHN NEAL

WAY, THE *See also:* ZEN

Without going out of doors one may know the whole world. Without looking out of the window, one may see The Way of Heaven. The further one travels the less one may know. Thus it is that without moving you shall know, without looking you shall see, without doing you shall achieve.   ▶LAO-TSE

WEALTH *See also:* POVERTY

The advantages of wealth are greatly exaggerated.   ▶LELAND STANFORD

We all covet wealth, but not its perils.   ▶JEAN DE LA BRUYÈRE

Riches are gotten with pain, kept with care, and lost with grief. The cares of riches lie heavier upon a good man than the inconveniences of an honest poverty.   ▶SIR ROGER L'ESTRANGE

WEATHER

Sunshine is delicious, rain is refreshing, wind braces up, snow is exhilarating; there is really no such thing as bad weather, only different kinds of good weather.   ▶JOHN RUSKIN

WHITEWATER

Reputation, reputation, reputation! Oh, I have lost my reputation. I have lost the immortal part of myself, and what remains is bestial.
▶SHAKESPEARE

Be thou as chaste as ice, as pure as snow, thou shalt not escape calumny. ▶SHAKESPEARE

WINDOWS OF OPPORTUNITY

But, soft! What light through yonder window breaks? ▶SHAKESPEARE

The secret of success in life is for a man to be ready for his opportunity when it comes. ▶BENJAMIN DISRAELI

WINE

The use of wine must inevitably be a stepping-stone to that of stronger drinks and to intemperance. ▶J. C. HOLBROOK

Wine is a noble, generous liquor, and we should be humbly thankful for it, but, as I remember, water was made before it. ▶JOHN ELIOT

WINTER

In the midst of winter, I finally learned that there was in me an invincible summer. ▶ALBERT CAMUS

WISDOM

More helpful than all wisdom is one draught of simple human pity that will not forsake us. ▶GEORGE ELIOT

Be wiser than other people if you can; but do not tell them so.
▶LORD CHESTERFIELD

We become wiser by adversity: prosperity destroys our appreciation of the right. ▶SENECA

Nothing can be truer than fairy wisdom. It is as true as sunbeams.
▶DOUGLAS JERROLD

The wise man is he who knows the relative value of things.
▶DEAN WILLIAM R. INGE

The riddle of the ages has for each a private solution. ▶EMERSON

WISHING AND WISHFUL THINKING

Wishes, like castles in the air, are inexpensive and not taxable.

▶THOMAS C. HALIBURTON

If a man could have half his wishes he would double his troubles.

▶BEN FRANKLIN

WOE AND WORRY

No scene of human life but teems with mortal woe.

▶SIR WALTER SCOTT

Worry is interest paid on trouble before it becomes due.

▶DEAN WILLIAM R. INGE

As a cure for worrying, work is better than whiskey.

▶THOMAS EDISON

WOKS

Whatever your recipe, whether for fish or fowl, the most important ingredient is timing. Like a kiss at the wrong moment, a pinch of ginger may destroy a marriage, or even the kingdom of a thousand years.

▶WON WAH

WOMEN

In all societies women have played a much more important role than their menfolk are generally ready to admit. ▶Ashley Montagu

WORDS AND WORD PROCESSING

A thousand words will not leave so deep an impression as one deed. ▶Henrik Ibsen

WORK ETHIC, THE

If idleness does not produce vice or malevolence, it commonly produces melancholy. ▶Sydney Smith

I doubt if hard work, steadily and regularly carried on, ever yet hurt anybody. ▶Lord Stanley

They say hard work never hurt anybody, but I figure—why take the chance? ▶President Ronald Reagan

I like work; it fascinates me. I can sit and look at it for hours.
▶Jerome K. Jerome

WRINKLES *See also*: MOONLIGHT

The wrinkles of the heart are more indelible than those of the brow.
▶DOROTHÉE DELUZY

Politeness smooths wrinkles. ▶JOSEPH JOUBERT

To be happy, we must be true to nature, and carry our age along with us. ▶WILLIAM HAZLITT

XEROX™

It is far better to be an original of yourself than a copy of even the latest dandy among the smart set of Mayfair or Piccadilly.

▶Beau Cavendish

X-RATED *See also*: profit motive, the

We have all a propensity to grasp at forbidden fruit.

▶Ralph Cudworth

Recommend virtue to your children. Only that will make them happy, and certainly not gold.   ▶Beethoven

X RAYS

For every bad there might be a worse; and when one breaks his leg, let him be thankful it was not his neck.   ▶Bishop Joseph Hall

XYLOPHONES

Music washes away from the soul the dust of everyday life.

▶Berthold Auerbach

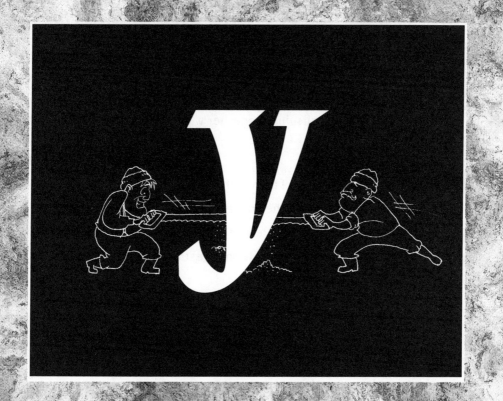

YACHTS *See also*: EXECUTIVE PERKS

Wealth is the least trustworthy of anchors.   ▶J. G. HOLLAND

YEARNINGS

Unless you're an heir to at least an earldom, yearnings without earnings are as useless as pursuing a poacher when your foot is bandaged with the gout.   ▶SIR JOHN RUTLEDGE

YOUTH

Keep true to the dreams of thy youth.   ▶SCHILLER

Youth lasts far longer than the young imagine.   ▶COMTESSE DIANE

In youth we learn; in age we understand.   ▶MARIE EBNER-ESCHENBACH

Youth is eminently the fittest season for establishing habits of industry.   ▶DR. FARR

There is a feeling of Eternity in youth which makes us amends for everything. To be young is to be as one of the immortals.   ▶HAZLITT

Youth is a wonderful thing. What a crime to waste it on children.
    ▶GEORGE BERNARD SHAW

ZABAGLIONE See also: APPLES

There are men whose stomachs are the clamorous creditors that sooner or later throw them into bankruptcy. ▶BASFORD

ZEBRAS

Even when Nature can't make up her mind about one of her creatures, the result is always interesting. ▶LADY MINNY LESTER

ZEN

Zen enriches no one. ▶THOMAS MERTON

Let us be silent that we may hear the whispers of the gods. ▶EMERSON

ZODIAC, THE

Whither the fates lead, virtue will follow without fear. ▶LUCAN

ZOMBIES

If we're too lazy or stupid to think for ourselves, a thousand leaders will be happy to do it for us. They will, of course, exact their usual fee— our souls. ▶BARON VON GUERSTER

ZOOS *See also*: TALK SHOWS

The orangutan teaches us that looks aren't everything—but darned near it. ▶WILL CUPPY

All animals know that the ultimate purpose of life is to enjoy it.
▶SAMUEL BUTLER

ZYGOTES

There is no cure for birth or death save to enjoy the interval.
▶GEORGE SANTAYANA

THE END

All's well that ends well. ▶SHAKESPEARE